I have read your manuscript and I really enjoyed your reminiscences ... perhaps because I could relate to many of them in my own life. My feeling is that you have captured the essence of an era that deserves to be remembered. There are times when your readers will be moved to tears; and times when they will be delighted by great smiles. I congratulate you on this accomplishment, and wish you good luck in the completion of this project.

Dr. H. B. Hardy
Retired Administrator
University of Central Arkansas


I have had the good fortune to "come along" with you for part of my life. Many of the things you stand for we share — family, friends and faith. You have captured the spirit of the important things about life in this book. Let us sing on together!

Dr. Harold L. "Hal" Lewis
Experimental Scientist
Arkansas Agriculture Hall of Fame

# Come With Me

Joe D. Ward

ISBN 978-0-615-30894-4

Written and published by Joe D. Ward
Edited by John L. Ward
Produced by Bill M. Ward — www.billwardphotography.com
Designed by Emelene Russell — www.emelene.com

To contact the author and publisher or to order additional copies of this book:

Joe D. Ward
27 Bluebird Lane
Conway, AR 72032

Email: wardbldg@cyberback.com

# Acknowledgements

I have received many special blessings in my life, and I am thankful for every one. One such blessing has been the enhanced relationship with my two remaining brothers over the past five years. In that period we have been together an average of twice a week, to visit, eat, plan, work, cut wood, whatever we could do together we did.

They are both experienced authors, and a few months ago they decided that this book should be published. They took it over, made plans, and decided that we had to have a "book meeting" every Friday morning following breakfast. After sixteen weeks, thirty five pounds of ham and two hundred eighty-eight biscuits we got it all together.

So to John and Bill go the credit for the completion of this project. And to my wife, Dena, the credit for inspiring me and making me believe that what I had written would be good reading for someone else.

Joe D. Ward

# Contents

# Come With Me

Come with me and share my memories and thoughts. Come and share my stories of my ancestors and the people who helped raise me and understand my respect for their character and the way they lived.

Come with me and share the wonder of Nature that God has provided.

Come with me on a warm summer afternoon and we'll go to the bottom of a deep hollow where there is a spring. We'll clean it out, watch the water clear then get a drink of the cool, clear water.

Come with me and share my love for my family, for my wife of fifty-five years, my children, grandchildren and great grandchildren.

Come with me and share my love for my extended family, and my sadness when I think of those who have passed on.

Come with me and share my life now with my two remaining brothers who live near the cabin on the road that our ancestors traveled.

Come with me on the first really crisp Fall day with a light wind from the north, bring your bucket and we will fill it with big purple muscadines. After we eat all we want, we'll make a few jars of jelly.

Come with me and be inspired to write your own memories and stories for yourself and for those who will come after you. It is true that everyone has a story.

Our family today is a large, diverse group of about 60 people. We range in age up to 80-plus. We live in ten states, from ultra urban to deep woods. We range politically from ultra conservative to ultra liberal. Our professions are as varied as our philosophies. Our religions vary from Baptist to Methodist, Lutheran, Catholic, and the church of the open sky.

# The Family

With all these differences, we still come together in love and unity and function as the largest, closest family that I know. We have seen our children and grandchildren grow up and leave, and we have seen their desire to be a part of all this and have seen them cancel almost any other engagement to be with the family, especially at special times like the Ward Family Christmas.

So where does this closeness come from? Not from Dad, who, though he loved his sisters and brothers-in-law, certainly didn't make a big effort to get together with them. And Mother had one step-sister who died a long time ago, so it didn't come from her. To my knowledge, Grandfather and Grandmother never made any particular effort to see their brothers and sisters, so it didn't come from them, and I never remember Grandfather Richardson even mentioning his brothers. So this closeness was not in our heritage, it wasn't from example.

We could probably say that we caused it, at least in part. We began the Ward Family Christmas in 1973, and that has had an effect. Our singing, which has been accepted in such a wonderful way, has been a part of it also, but it still does not explain the chemistry. A part of it is the way we treat each other with respect for opinions and beliefs. We don't argue religion or politics. Alcohol is not consumed at our gatherings, so no one gets drunk and says things they might later regret. The loss of two brothers, especially the death of Bobby who was so connected to family, and the awareness of our own mortality have had a part in it also. However, I don't think these things are the total answer. Bill thinks that the singing has been the most important factor, since we all had to be together so much. That is certainly an important part, but I think that it still doesn't explain the chemistry.

Renee (granddaughter of Mom and Dad) thinks that the chemistry probably began with them. She was impressed at an early age with the closeness of the siblings, and I think that may very well have been the beginning. I think we can say that Mother and Dad were responsible for that. Of course, I can remember hating my siblings, particularly my older brothers, and vowing to get even when I was big enough, but all brothers go through that.

Another aspect of the family has been the attraction to it from non-related people. As I look at old pictures of the family Christmas gatherings, I see many of these people that have been a part of the gatherings through the years. The family has the ability to make them feel they are a part of it all. Some have been with us for a number of years, and new ones are added almost every year.

One thought keeps coming to my mind, and that is it began with Mother. She loved her family in a special way. How she loved for the children to come home! I can see her face now when we would arrive. It seemed that her smile touched both ears. And when we would leave, we took the smile with us.

I remember her feelings soon after the eldest children, Marketa and Loweta, were married. Any time they were coming home became the most exciting times for all of us. Mother would plan for days in advance what she would cook, where everyone would sleep, wanting everything to be perfect.

My mother—an intelligent, attractive, artistic young lady, who gave up her potential as a leader in any field to become a supporter, a background person, the wind beneath her husband's wings. She was the most unselfish person I've ever known. And the sad thing to me is that I didn't recognize this great trait of hers until she was gone.

As best we can tell, the story of Old House began about 1850. Mr. William Johnson came and homesteaded the land, then began to make the necessary improvements to "prove up" the place. I can only imagine what the place looked like when he first saw it. All of the valley would have been solid in virgin timber, mostly oak and a few pines. He would have started cutting trees near the place he had chosen for the house first. Then he would have moved on

# The Story of Old House

down towards the branch, choosing red oak and white oak for the logs for the house, cutting and burning the brush as he went first for a place for a garden and then fields to plant. He would have needed about 70 logs for the house itself and probably 12 for the floor (though he may have waited on the floor, using the dirt floor for a few years). The ceiling joists would have been smaller trees, and would have required a post or two in the middle of the room, since it was almost 20 feet square. The rafters would have been even smaller. Then he would have cut blocks from red oak to split shingles for the roof. He probably made his own nails at his forge and anvil, and I'm sure he didn't waste any. The window holes wouldn't have had glass in them, and they would have hung animal skins to keep out as much weather as they could.

He used surface rocks for the foundation, but used quarried rocks for the chimney. I don't know where he found a place to dig out these rocks, but somewhere nearby. They are amazingly uniform in thickness. He chose a beautiful place for the house, protected on the north by a hill and high enough above the branch that it would never flood. According to handed down oral history, this valley he chose was noted for its many honey bees and fat bears.

He probably lived in his wagon while he was building his house and lived off the land, spending as much time as necessary hunting and gathering.

I like to think he arrived in the early spring and started clearing, building and planting something to eat. His crops and his garden would have been just as important as anything he would have done.

I don't know anything about how much help he had, how close his neighbors were, what the roads were like or what the weather was like that year. I can only imagine the difficulties he faced.

I think about the fall of that year. I hope he raised lots of vegetables and food for his stock. It would have taken him most of the summer to build his house, and I like to think they moved into it sometime in the late fall, perhaps just ahead of the first really cold front of the winter. The rains would have been ahead of the front, and they listened to the wind and rain as they sat around the fireplace, feeling safe and secure in their solid, well-built home.

My father said that William Johnson planted the two pecan trees in the yard, one of which is still living. The other one died in the last few years. He was apparently a good farmer and substantial citizen of the community, for he was appointed postmaster of Bee Branch in 1866 and had the post office in his home. My father and grandfather always referred to the farm as the Johnson place.

Grandfather John T. Ward bought the place in 1910 or very close to that date. They moved in the late fall and discovered that the family who had lived there that summer had planted late potatoes but didn't harvest them. Grandfather plowed them up, and the kids gathered a washtub full. What a wonderful gift! I suppose that most of the fields they farmed were cleared, though Dad did talk about clearing and then plowing in a new ground. Cotton was their money crop, although it was difficult to grow enough for a bale on the poor hillsides. When they had a bale, Grandfather would take it in the wagon to Morrilton and sell it, buy the things they had to have and hope for a better crop next year. Grandfather was a good sorghum maker and possibly made a little money from this. I have seen where he had his cooking pans down by the branch.

By this time they were a family of nine and were out of room in the house. Grandfather and his brother-in-law, Will Sims, cut pine trees off the farm and hauled them to a sawmill where they were cut into lumber. They then built the kitchen and "ell" room onto the original log house. This more than doubled the size of the house, and I'm sure it was a wonderful feeling for Grandmother and all the kids.

William Johnson had dug a well just east of the house, and that was their source of water until Aunt Flaura developed typhoid fever and the doctor told them the well was probably the source. So they drilled a well on the west side.

Though they had a well, Grandmother chose to do most of their washing at the branch south of the house. She had her wash pot down there, and they would wash the clothes, then hang them on bushes to dry.

There were two apple trees growing between the house and the branch, and Grandfather always planted his wheat around them. There was a flour mill at Quitman, and Dad said that when they would run out of flour, grandmother would cook cornbread for breakfast, so the wheat was very important. When Aunt Flaura had typhoid, the only treatment was simply not to let the patient eat anything. One day when the rest of the family was at work in the fields, she went to the apple trees and ate apples which almost killed her.

There were so many memories that Dad had of the place that I can't record all of them here. When he took me to the farm the first time, I wasn't really impressed with it. It was an old, run-down house and barn and a lot of grown-up fields, but he could make it come alive with his stories.

He was born in 1902 in a house on the other side of the branch, then moved to the old house in about 1909 or 1910. He spent his formative years here from about eight to 18 and those memories were always with him. Dad was a strong-minded Baptist preacher, so we moved a lot. I was living in my ninth house when I was married and left to begin my own home. We were always blessed with a secure, loving home, but the house we kept it in kept changing. As a result of this moving, we siblings never had a place we called our home place. The old house where Dad grew up was home to him, so we adopted it as our home place as well. We called it simply "Old House."

Soon after that first trip, Dad announced that he had bought the place. The house had three rooms downstairs, two upstairs and a hallway separating the living room and the "ell" room. It had a barn and 496 acres of land. The house needed a lot of work to make it livable, and we started work on it the next spring. We cut trees in an area across the branch, pulled the logs out with an old F-12 Farmall tractor and sent them to Shofner sawmill in Damascus. This was the lumber we used to add three rooms to the house the next summer.

Dad sent Uncle Elzey along with John, Bob, and me to remodel the house that summer. Between fishing trips, swimming trips and ball games, we finally got the house in livable condition. Uncle Elzey and Aunt Irene moved into the house in the late summer, then they moved back to Bigelow and we moved into the house in the late fall of 1950. Sometime that winter, Dad moved Grandfather and Grandmother Ward in with us because Grandfather was very sick.

We remember that winter as a harsh one with lots of snow. We spent the entire winter out of firewood which may have affected our memory of just how harsh the winter was. Our job every Saturday or holiday was to cut and split firewood. It wouldn't have been such a chore if we had had the equipment we have now, but then it was a cross-cut saw and an axe, and really slow. Grandfather died the last day of February 1951 at the age of 77.

The next summer we moved to another pastorate for a few months, then back to Damascus. Dad still owned the place for a while, then sold it. I tried to borrow the money from a bank to buy it myself, and they were nice to me, explaining that I was 17 years old and not a really good credit risk.

For the next few years the man Dad sold the place to lived there. When he moved away we used the house for a camp house. In 1958, I leased the place and moved back from New Mexico. Mother and Dad had fixed up the house to make it livable, and we moved in. My wife and I enjoyed the late summer and early fall kind of camping, taking our baths in the creek, but when it got cold, we bought a farm about a mile up the road, put in running water and a bath room and moved in.

The following spring our house burned, and we moved to Conway. We still used Old House for a camp house. Dad would come up in September on his birthday and camp and squirrel hunt, and we had some good times.

In 1969, I broke both my legs in a construction accident and got to know my orthopedist over the next few months. I told him about the old farm, which was now owned by a bank in Louisiana, and he bought it with the agreement that I would take care of it. I took care of it for the next 15 years, going there almost every Friday night. We raised our children during this period, and most weekends would find Joey hunting or fishing, or Mica bringing a bunch of girls for a bunking party. Joey's friends grew up there too, some of them spending about as much time as I did. Sometime in the mid-80s, the owner's son got old enough to have a deer camp there, so we abandoned it. A few years later, Deltic Timber owned it, and I asked them if I could have the house, tear it down and move it. They agreed, but I didn't have a place to build it back.

It is gone now, reduced to a pile of rubble by a back hoe in September of 2005. As I sit here reflecting on it, I can see the firelight from my fireplace reflecting off the logs that I used for my mantle and the hearth rock that I took from the fireplace. Above the mantle is the painting of that old house that Dena and I commissioned more than 40 years ago. To the right is Grandfather Ward's dog horn and Bobby's poem, "Home." Although these parts and pieces bring floods of memories, they can never replace "Old House."

I'm sure the builders of the house, William Johnson, Grandfather Ward and my father, never expected nor even imagined that their building would last as long as it has.

In its lifetime, it saw births and heard the laughter of children, it saw periods of prosperity when crops were good and hunger and depression when they were bad, and it saw times of happiness and times of sickness and death.

It lives in our memories.

A gathering of Ward family members at Old House. Several are gone now

The old wood-burning stove cranked out plenty of good food when it dominated the kitchen at Old House

Dear Bob:
To say I have had
a good time would
not begin to tell of
John and I came up
monday — As you know
I had a birthday yester.
(59).
Joe came up yester
We had squirrel ste
last night — There is
Just no place like
the "Johnston Place
Hope John will
send you some
pictures --
Hope it will not
be long untill you
all can Join us
again,
Dad.

Dad's note to Bob says it all on his 59th birthday

**A**s I reflect today on Old House, I begin to see more of what it means, or what it meant, since it is gone now. In Dena's introduction to "The Spirit of Old House," she said that my passion for this house is more than log, mortar, stone and tin, that it was a symbol of family and values. She is right, of course, but I have come to believe that it is even more than that. To me, now, it is a symbol of the society that inhabited the house and the area at the time of my father's birth and the years immediately following.

# A New Look at Old House

Today I arrived in the community in an air-conditioned, comfortable truck, entered my cabin, turned on the lights and adjusted the thermostat for the temperature I wanted. I rinsed my hands in hot water at the sink, laid a fire in the fireplace and lit it, mostly just for looks, with wood that I cut with a chain saw and split with a power splitter. I put some ham hocks in a pan, added water and started it cooking on the electric range. As I think about these things that I did, I can't help but think about what life was like for my ancestors. Any of these things would have been so foreign to their knowledge and experience that they could not even dream of them.

I think first about comfort, how easily the cabin can be warmed. When we had the use of Old House, I remember being there when the weather was really cold and trying to stay warm. We would build as big a fire as the fireplace would hold, and would keep it going all the time we were there. I remember that the snow we had tracked in would not melt on the floor six feet away from the fireplace. This was after I had re-chinked the logs, sealed around the windows and insulated the attic. I asked Aunt Era one time how they stayed warm. She said Grandmother would card and spin wool and make underwear for them, then they would wear all their clothes. Thinking about wool underwear makes me itch all over.

A great luxury my grandparents had in later years was a wood range for the kitchen. This stove would put out a great deal of heat when really fired up, so the kitchen became the place to get warm. Of course it had the opposite effect in the summer when it still had to be fired up to cook and can on.

This morning at daylight as I watched the birds and squirrels in their search for food, I thought how much like our ancestors they are. When they awake, their first thoughts are for food and water. Basic life functions. Survival in an uncertain world. Grandmother's first thoughts upon awakening would have been food for her family. Preparations would have begun the day before or several days before, or months before. If it was in the winter like today, preparations would have begun last Spring, when they got some pigs to raise and fatten out. They would have butchered these in late Fall and cured and smoked the meat and canned the sausage. Back in the Spring they would have encouraged some of their hens to set on their eggs and raise some chicks which now might be laying an occasional egg. They would have harvested their wheat with a cradle, tied it into bundles and stacked it until it was dry. When it was dry, they would beat the grains off, blow the dust and chaff out, bag it up and take it to the miller for the flour she would use for biscuits.

They would have raised their sorghum, and Grandfather would have made syrup in the early Fall. They would have churned some of the milk they got from their cows each day, and they would have had butter. If the cotton crop had been good enough, they would have bought some things like a bag of coffee beans. They would have roasted these, then each morning Grandfather would grind enough for their morning coffee. Grandmother might open a jar of sausage, shake it into a skillet and fry it and then make gravy to go with the biscuits. Dad said what woke him up each morning was the sound of coffee being ground and other sounds of breakfast, like the shaking out of the sausage.

After breakfast, she would have begun preparing lunch while the stove was still hot. Turnips and greens would probably still be available, but if not, there would be turnips in the storage pit and potatoes under the house. Cornbread would be their principal bread, since it was something they could provide. They would select the best ears of corn in the crib, shell it and take it to a local mill for it to be ground into meal. The man who ground it would take as payment a small amount of the meal.

January 15, 1912

    Ida awakened to the sound of John building a fire in the kitchen stove. She hadn't heard him stirring up the fire in the fireplace and adding kindling and wood. She got up and put on her clothes over her long underwear to begin the day. Her first thoughts were for breakfast for the family. John would grind the coffee beans and make the coffee as soon as the stove got hot. She hoped that Roy had drawn a bucket of water before he went to bed like he had been told. John would be upset if he had forgotten. She enjoyed these times when it was just the two of them, and hoped that he wouldn't be upset. At these times, they talked mostly about the children, all six of them. They had lost two, but they seldom discussed them. Sometimes he would want to talk about world conditions and politics and about Andrew Carnegie and his putting a hundred twenty-five million dollars into a charitable trust. She couldn't imagine having a hundred twenty-five dollars and sure couldn't imagine millions. She was a little tired this morning, Era had had an earache in the night and kept her up for a while. With six children, it seemed that at least one of them would have some problem every night.

    She would like to get John to thinking about their girls. Maggie was sixteen, Don fourteen and Flaura twelve, and she knew they were thinking about boys. Ida knew that John would say they were too young to be thinking about boys, but they weren't and she knew it. She remembered how she thought at that age.

    The kitchen range had warmed the room by the time she got there, and she paused a moment to offer a prayer of thanks for her stove. John had the coffee pot on one of the burners, and she put her large iron skillet on another and went to the closet for a jar of sausage. She shook this into the skillet and got her bread bowl and proceeded to make biscuits while John went to call the kids. Although she had plenty of flour, she couldn't help but ration it when she remembered last year when they ran out in the late winter and didn't have any more until summer. How the kids complained about cornbread for breakfast.

    She heard Roy bouncing down the stairs and thought he probably didn't remember that this was a school day. As she made biscuits, she remembered to make enough extra for the kids' lunches. Maybe there would be a piece of sausage left for each of them also. She didn't get a chance to bring up the subject of the girls to John, with Roy in the kitchen and the girls beginning to come.

The temperature outside was well below freezing, but the kitchen was warming up nicely. John had built a big fire in the fireplace, but it didn't heat the living room. Everyone had to get dressed in their cold rooms, and they raced for the kitchen, sometimes with only half their clothes on. "Lula Elmus, you go take that dress off and put on that gray one, you can't wear your Sunday dress to school, you know that." "But, Momma, that is one of Maggie's old dresses and everyone at school knows it." "That don't matter, go change." Flaura said, "It's just because of that new boy at school." Elmus shouted back as she went to change that it wasn't true, she just wanted to look nice. "Roy, you can wear those overalls today, but you better remember to change when you get home." A guilty thought crossed her mind then. The girls were always saying that she was partial to Roy, and she knew it was true. He was her only boy now. Jimmy Clayton had died two years ago at about this same time.

"Flaura Jane, you don't get any milk for breakfast, you'll have to drink water. I saw you scaring the cows yesterday with that old umbrella, and they wouldn't give their milk down last night." Flaura blushed and dropped her head, thought about denying the charge, but quickly gave up that idea. She thought no one had seen her, and it was fun watching old Bossy with her tail high in the air running as fast as she could. John didn't say anything. He just looked at her, which was message enough. They all finally gathered at the table, John offered thanks and they had breakfast.

And so the day began. The children would go to school, John would hook up the team to the wagon and haul in firewood. It seemed like there would never be enough. They had piled the wood high in the Fall, but it was about gone now with winter just beginning. He untied old Roy and Singer and took his gun along with the thought that they might tree a squirrel or run a rabbit by him. Ida would spend the day preparing food for supper, something for their dinner, and patching up some of the children's clothes.

They didn't complain about their lot in life. There was no one to complain to, for all their relatives and neighbors were in the same situation they were. They had faith that God would provide everything they needed, and their part was to work as hard as they could, which they did every day.

The boys readying to hunt: Barry, Tony, Joey, Tim and Brian; Bill, Joe and John

Three brothers
and three boys
at Old House

The seven
surviving
children of
Roy and
Mamie Ward.
Only five
left now.
Made in
Fargo during
a visit with
Bob and Jo

**I** had felt like I would somehow know when it was the right time to remove the life support system and let her go. Now was the time. It had been a lot of trouble to just keep her going the last couple of years. It took a lot of time and energy and some money. She wasn't needed as much anymore either. And she was getting pretty old. Her youngest part was over 40 years old now. So it was time to pull the plug.

# Restoring Old House for One More Year

The decision was practical. When I told Joey, he understood, but managed to let me know that somehow, someway Old House should always be there. Others both in and out of the family all reacted about the same way. So I decided to try to put her together one more time for one more year.

I put out the word that I was going up there today if anyone should want to come and help. John was in Mexico, Barry in law school, Tim and Tony off somewhere on tour, Joey already committed to working for his boss, the Logan boys working, Roe Henderson working, a slight possibility that Jim Henderson might come, Bill Ward was wherever advertising executives go when there is work to be done, so that I felt like I would have lots of privacy. I did.

I arrived at seven with a load of lumber a friend had given, a box of nails and a saw. I went first to the spring for water and made a pot of coffee. While the coffee was dripping I heard a hawk scream in the west pecan tree and slipped out to the breezeway and watched as it flew down near the branch and joined its mate driving off two other hawks from its territory. I wondered how it could tell its mate from the others since they all looked alike, but it didn't seem to have any trouble.

The magnitude of the needed repairs almost overwhelmed me. Then I remembered that a journey of a thousand miles, etc., and started on the back porch. It had reached the point where I wasn't sure that I could remember where not to step, so it was a good place to start. The lumber the friend had given was two by sixes, so that was what the porch should be built of. As I opened my tool box, the two tools on top were the level and square. I put them aside out of the way, knowing they wouldn't be needed. A builder must always remember the importance of architectural integrity. With a level and square this project might be in jeopardy.

I tore off the whole porch, thinking what good kindling the aged pine would make. I built the framework of joists, thinking that the rocks piled up for the corner pier should be properly laid in mortar, then remembering architectural integrity, I stacked them up the way they were before. I thought briefly about the level again, then decided it would be better to wait for rain and see if the water ran off. I floored the porch, agonized a few minutes about the irregular front edge, got a chalk line and the saw and cut it straight. I replaced the posts, put the water bucket shelf that uncle Elzie built back at the end and added rails. I thought about a Chippendale design then remembered integrity and promptly forgot it. Took a cane bottom chair out, leaned it against the wall, put my feet on the rail and drank the rest of the coffee.

Went next to the front where some of the tin had blown completely off and a lot of it was loose. As I was starting on this, Jim Henderson came and we nailed the roof back down. We then tore off the front porch, which had been patched 11 times. We put down the framework of joists, eyeballed them for level and decided we would have to wait for some one-inch lumber to floor it with, since we were out of two by sixes.

I hadn't taken anything to eat, and the thieves who had taken everything that was edible two weeks before left our shelves bare except for a can of green beans that looked like it might explode if disturbed. So we went up to John and Bill's ranch hungry. We found a can of dumplings with gravy, three frozen cooked pork chops and two Cokes. We took them, had a good lunch, decided someone else could move the scrap lumber, changed a flat tire on my truck and came home.

So now with the flooring boards for the front porch, a little tar for the roof, she should last out the year. At least the back porch will. I decided on the way home that perhaps John had helped the most by being in Mexico. He has an obsession with levels and squares that does not co-exist with the architectural integrity of Old House.

The Ward Family Christmas began soon after the death of our parents in the early 1970s. It was an effort to help hold a large, close family together. The old house near where they last lived, where Dad grew up, was available to us, so this was the place.

We have met there every year except one when the roads were iced and we couldn't get there. We usually meet a day or two after Christmas.

# Ward Family Christmas 1990

I don't think anyone remembers who had the idea to exchange handmade gifts, but now everyone is sure the idea was theirs. We began about 15 years ago. We draw names at Christmas and exchange gifts the following Christmas, so we have a full year to conceive the idea and create the gift. As in any group this size, there are 47 of us now, there are some who start on their gift in January and others who must put wet paint signs on their gift which was finished the night before the exchange.

The gifts are as varied as the people who make them. There are funny ones that one brother creates—like nailing together three blocks of wood and calling it modern sculpture entitled, "Gunfight at the OK Corral." The out-of-state brother usually does an oil painting or a carved work of art, and everyone hopes all year that he has their name. There are photographs from the past, cross-stitched pieces, furniture, a stuffed bear made from my children's cast-off clothes, jellies, jams, a load of firewood, gifts made from craft kits, etc. However great or small it may be, the knowledge that this gift was created just for you makes it immediately become special.

Perhaps we have found the true spirit of giving at this special time of the year. I have seen the children when they were small being concerned only with what they would get. I see them now as young adults being concerned with the response to the gift they give. I have seen the glow on their faces when the recipient of their gift is touched with their effort. I have also seen the way they will cancel almost any other plans in order to be there on that day.

We have added things through the years. Some have become traditions and we keep those. Others we have dropped. For a few years, we had a touch football game. Then, as we grew older and our kids grew up, we found that we couldn't compete with them—so we quit.

We gather at the house all through the morning, some of the ones who arrive first go to the woods and cut a tree, we set it up, decorate it and then place the gifts under it. While this is going on, Jenifer serves her stollen and we drink coffee.

We place a chair where all can see and call out the names on the gift. The person receiving sits in the chair and opens his or her gift. We continue until all the gifts are shared. Finally, we get into as much of a circle as we can in the small room and sing a couple of carols and end by singing Auld Lang Syne. Then we all go up to the ranch for our big meal.

Many things contribute to the joy we feel on this day:

The season itself which causes us all to feel a little less selfish perhaps.

A large family that is very close.

The members of the group who are not related but who have become family over the  years.

Memories of some who are no longer with us.

The old house with its log room that served first as the Bee Branch post office in the Civil War and which holds so many memories.

Wanting to grasp and hold on to each moment, knowing that the group as it is can't last forever.

Wondering if the tradition is strong enough that our children and grandchildren will continue it.

All this and more make Ward Family Christmas special!

Whe have been singing all our lives. Our father was our pastor and he insisted on it. If you were a child of Roy W. Ward, you sang, and if you could walk un-assisted you went to the choir. To make sure you knew the basics of music, Dad always arranged for a singing school in the summer, usually taught by R.H. McNew, and sometimes by Wallace Glover or Richard Smith. At

# Ward Family Singers

these schools we were exposed to the latest gospel songs in the Stamps-Baxter books that were published each year, then we would listen to the radio anytime we could, hoping that we would hear one of our favorites. The Stamps quartet and The Stamps-Baxter Melody Boys were the groups in our area, and we would go to their concerts anytime we could, then we would try to sing like they did.

When we grew up and married, almost all of us chose mates who were musically inclined, and some of them extremely talented. Without them, our musical performances would have just been for our own enjoyment.

Anytime we were at home to visit, Dad would plan some kind of special singing for us to present at church. When they lived at Nashville and Dad was pastor of Immanuel Baptist Church, Gary, our youngest sibling, would sometimes record our efforts. Gary had a deep, resonant bass voice and loved to sing. He was a licensed minister, and after working all night as a disc jockey in Little Rock, he was critically injured in an automobile accident the next morning and died a few weeks later just before his 21st birthday.

No one knows how many times we sang as a group, mostly for funerals. We all got together at Mom and Dad's in 1968 and made an album. John obtained the services of Steve Jaggers, who brought his recording equipment to Old Euseba Church, and we spent a few hours recording. We only ordered 15 or so albums which he made individually on a hot stylus machine. Bill made a picture of us in front of the little church and that became the album cover. Naturally, Mom and Dad thought that it was the finest album ever made. We made another the next year, again just enough copies for the family.

Whenever we all were together someone would say, "Let's sing some." We kept enough *Heavenly Highway Hymns* and *Favorite Songs* books, and would sing sometimes for an hour or two. We talked a lot then about making a serious album, but never got serious about it.

Then in 1991 we were all shocked into reality when Bobby died of a heart attack on September 15. All our plans for making an album included Bobby. He had a wonderful, well- trained voice, and no one loved to sing any more than he did. The year before he died, the siblings all went to Fargo and spent the weekend. They didn't have a piano, so he instructed us to get Suzy to record some of the old favorites, then we would sing with that. He and Jo invited some friends over, and we sang all the old songs. What a wonderful time and wonderful memory.

Bill was always our director, and was director of advertising for the Ward Bus Company in Conway. That company was bought out by International Harvester, they had their own advertising department, so Bill went to work for Lifeword Broadcast Ministries. It was about this time that all the siblings moved to Conway. Lifeword began putting together some history of the Baptist Missionary Association, and wanted us to make an album for them, preserving the old songs that we had grown up with. We made this album, "Home," and they optimistically ordered 500 copies. This was in 1993, and to date they have distributed more than 4,000 copies.

A recording of Bobby singing "Some Golden Daybreak" was found and Bill incorporated it into that first album, with the family added to present it as a family rendition.

Two years later, we made another album, "Country Church," on our own, with money received in offerings when we gave concerts, and these continue to be distributed. When the family produced "Life Is Like A Mountain Railroad" in 2003, this would be our final studio recording project—though we did issue a "favorites" CD called "Sending You the Best" in 2005.

We gave our final concert on August 7, 2005, at Central Church to the largest audience the church had ever had.

During the past 15 years, we have given more than a hundred concerts, to audiences as small as 12 in a little Methodist church in Quitman and as large as 2,500 at the national meeting of the BMA of America. These concerts, mostly in

Arkansas, some in Mississippi and Oklahoma, have been very well received.

At first, I believe we were looking for our egos to be stroked and how much the offering was towards a chapel for the preservation and perpetuation of gospel music. Then a pastor at Morrilton said we were continuing the ministry that Daddy had started, and he gave an invitation at the end of the concert. I don't think I had thought about ministry much before. Now I believe that ministry is uppermost to most of us. Our concerts have been well received because we sing the old songs that appeal to a lot of people, and people see a large, loving family having fun on stage. This is something that we do, and it isn't an act. We aren't that good with acting that we could make believe we are having fun. It seems that a family as large as ours who get along with each other enough to rehearse and perform is rare these days, and this too is a ministry.

There have been many comments about the ministry of the recordings and the concerts, but I think the ministry has had its greatest effect on the family. We have always been a close loving family, but the necessity of being together so much, rehearsing, performing, traveling, eating, etc., has made a dramatic change in all of us. Someone kept up with the times we were together, and they totaled 68 in an 18-month period. Many families don't get together that many times in one person's lifetime.

These are my thoughts today, the day after the final big concert. First, I am tired and am here at the cabin to rest. All the activity on Saturday and all day yesterday really got to me, and I didn't do any of the physical things that I usually do for a concert. Next, I feel a great deal of satisfaction. The concert was not perfect, but we are not professional performers, and the people who came didn't come to see professionals, they came to see a family. As a family, it was one of our best concerts ever. It was satisfying to be able to finish a string of more than 100 concerts to a capacity crowd of very appreciative people. It was also wonderful to give our final concert before another of us was gone. It was wonderful to have my children be a part of it. Mica came and sang with us, and Joey and Teri and the kids came and were part of the dinner afterwards at Dixie Café. Finally, I feel sadness. It is sadness for me to see the end of an era, a time when the family grew closer to each other than ever before. I have treasured this closeness, and will never forget it. It is such a part of my life.

Despite the regrets I have, I am convinced that this was the time to end it. We thought we would end it last year at this time, and I thought then that it was time, but considering the developments this year, this was the proper time.

And so we reach the end of an important time in our lives. We had a lot of fun, spent so much time together, grew closer to each other and had an impact on thousands of people who came to our concerts and listened to us on tapes and CDs. A wonderful period of time that none of us will ever forget.

## The Children's Song

It could never seem right that the young should die,
  lives unlived—songs unsung—
  bright promise unfulfilled—in Earth's time.
We are left not knowing how to mourn a thing
  so out of pattern.
Grotesque  Unimaginable
But the gate of Heaven is open and
  God is ever there.
The children do not mourn. And the song they sing,
  we cannot hear, for we could not bear its sweetness.
But God hears them, and us, and the dark glass will clear in time.
We will see the whole design, and will marvel at the
  consuming rightness of it.
Face to face we will greet them, and they will sing us home.

Adapted from a poem by Bobby Ward
In the wake of the plane crash in Lockerbie, Scotland

**W**e hold title to only one acre, but we actually claim closer to a thousand acres. The only house we can see is on top of the hill to the south, about two miles away on the other side of our pond. It isn't our pond either, but we claim it too.

On this clear morning I have been sitting in the sun-room since six-fifteen. The first glimpse I have of the sun is at six-fifty, but it has been light since I first came out, and there has been a lot of activity already. The

# Springtime at the Homeplace

birds are so busy they haven't even time to sing. I just hear an occasional chirp. Spring has come and there is so much for them to do. Find a mate, build a nest, defend your territory if you are the male, lay the eggs if you are the female, locate good places to find food. Singing comes later I guess.

Big bird comes at six-thirty, to the far side of the pond today. He looks so awkward with his long ungainly looking legs and his extra long neck. He isn't though. When he sights a small fish, he coils his neck like a snake and shoots his head into the water and comes up with a fish. I haven't seen him miss yet. My granddaughter says that it really isn't Big Bird because it is gray and not yellow, but I don't change his name. He must have his mate on his mind, for he only catches one fish and leaves.

Mallard and his mate come next. I guess it is hard for them to slow down enough to make a soft landing. They hit the water and skid for five or six feet, then calmly swim to the shallow end of the pond. Fog began forming over the pond about six-thirty and is now making a little cloud that drifts slowly to the east.

Pileated lights on the big post oak nearest the house, making his piercing call that you can hear for a mile. He is really big. What fear must permeate a colony of bugs in a dead limb when he lights on it. With his jack-hammer bill he can demolish a dead limb in minutes, and as big as he is, it must take a lot of bugs to keep him going.

Pileated's cousin, Downy woodpecker, appears suddenly near the board fence on one of the post oaks. How nimble he is as he zips up the tree looking for bugs. He stops twice when he finds one.

Squirrel appears on the top limb of his den tree. He slipped out when I was watching the ducks I guess. He licks his paw, then wipes his eyes with it, performing his morning toilette. He had better be careful up there in full view. If Hawk should see him, he'll become Hawk's breakfast.

My mate comes out with her coffee, and I get a fresh cup for myself.

Two male summer tanagers appear on the north side of the sunroom, engaged in a bitter fight, probably over a mate or their territory. One hits the window and is knocked out. The other, thinking he has scored the big hit, flies down and starts pecking the other on the head, trying to kill him, I guess. My mate sends me out to break them up, the victor flies away and I pick up the vanquished and set him on my hand and carry him to the door. We can see the marks made by the other on his head and I place him on the porch where he stays for a while, then flies away, probably thinking that it is really a tough world out there.

A pair of robins land on the ground on the south side of the house and begin methodically moving the dead leaves, picking up each leaf and casting it aside, looking for bugs under them. Makes me feel better about not raking up the leaves.

Finally I hear a song from the male Carolina wren. They are building a nest in the woodpile, I think. He sits on the dead limb on the post oak and seems to stand on tip-toe to hit the really high notes of his song. The female looks up at him once and if I interpreted the look correctly, she wasn't giving him a look of adoration of his beautiful voice or his looks, but a look that said, "Get down here and help with this nest." But of course I'm not sure about that.

Hawk comes zipping through the trees so fast that I hardly get a look at him. I don't see how he gets through the trees, as fast as he is going.

Cardinal is singing now. I think they have a nest nearby, but I don't know for sure.

Mourning Dove is calling, I can't see him, but he is somewhere near the garden, and he isn't getting an answer. I mentally urge him to keep trying.

Bluebirds are sitting on the fence near the garden. I don't know where they nest, but they are here every year, and they don't use the box I built for them.

The fiddle head ferns all have their heads up in the proper shape, and the cinnamon ferns are about six inches tall.

Little gray birds, the male has a top knot, are now everywhere I look in the oak trees, catching bugs under the leaves.

If a hundred birds come to my glen each day, a conservative number, and they eat ten bugs each, also conservative, in just one year they will have consumed more than three hundred fifty thousand bugs, just from this one little area. That makes me more thankful for the birds.

A great get-together at Old House. Joe, Bob (with ever-present coffee cup), John and Bill

Celebrating Dad's birthday with coffee from a little furnace
on the bank of Indian Giver Pond

Dad with all his sisters.
As usual, he is not smiling

Joey with maybe
his first squirrel

Bobby, John and Joe
at Laurel, Mississippi

Our kids, Joey and Mica, about eight and four, came in all excited, wanting to have a Kool-Aid stand. We didn't really think it was such a good idea, but they were so excited about it that we decided to let them do it. They began their preparations at a run, not wanting to miss a single sale.

They found a box the right size to use for a table, got a chair from somewhere for Joey, who would be more or less in charge. They found **The Kool-Aid Stand** a small box to keep the money in, then while Dena and Mica made the Kool-Aid, Joey made the sign. KOOL-AID 5 CENTS.

Preparations all finally made, they waited for their first customer. But no one stopped. No one. For over an hour they waved at cars, pointed to the sign, acted like they were drinking it themselves and smiling, but no one stopped.

Mica caved in first. At this age, believing her daddy could fix anything, she came to me. Hardly able to talk, choking back sobs, she said, "Daddy, no one will stop, and we waved and pointed to the sign and everything, but they still won't stop." I told her that maybe it wasn't a good day for it, or maybe the people were in a hurry. I told her that the new highway with its 55-mile-per-hour speed limit wasn't really a good place, but she went back out, picked up her sign and started waving it again.

Desperately I tried to think of something I could do to ease the pain of their first big failure. I tried to call some friends and get them to come, but they weren't home. When I looked out I saw that even Joey was ready to give up, his big brown eyes beginning to fill with tears. And then a miracle happened! A car stopped.

It was going so fast that it couldn't stop at the driveway and it went a long way past and then backed up into our driveway. The doors opened and the two got out. I believe they were the dirtiest, greasiest, long-haired hippies I had ever seen. Their clothes looked like they hadn't been off their filthy bodies in months. My conservative blood began to boil and I started for the door, and then I saw my children's faces and stopped. These hippies, who had in a moment become All American Boys drank their much weakened Kool-Aid, insisted that it was worth at least a quarter, thanked the kids for having a stand there just when they needed it, got into their old car and drove off.

If I could have caught them, I would have hugged them, dirt, grease, long hair and all.

1968: Dad is a Rockefeller campaign director in Van Buren County, and visiting with Lieutenant Governor Footsie Britt

**N**eeds Creek was a community similar to hundreds of others in the south. Rural, farming, primarily row crop, with cotton as the money crop. It was a place and a time when the whole family was involved in working the fields, a place where the gardens and truck patches were just as important as the cotton. A place where most families ate what they produced, spent the summer canning and preserving food for the winter and

# Life at Needs Creek in the Forties

hoped for a good cotton crop. Most of the people borrowed money from a bank to put in the crop, then hoped that there would be enough crop to pay off the bank, and maybe a little left over. The community had a school until 1938, when it was consolidated with Greenbrier. After this, the church was the center of the community.

We built what to us was this huge house just north of the church on the land where the school had been. The house had almost sixteen hundred square feet for the nine of us who lived there. Plus we had an inside bath, the only house so equipped between Springhill and Holland. I think we moved there in '47, but I spent a lot of time in the community before we moved.

The church was unique in several ways. All the people were called by their first names. Sam and Ruth, Jack and Jessie Lee, Russell and Una, Shep and Mildred, Fat and Gwen, Zack and Clara, Cecil and Eva, Coy and Edna, Haskell and Jo, Slim and Sis, Ted and Grace, Jess and Myrtle, and on and on. The older ones would have Uncle or Aunt attached, Uncle Jesse and Aunt Carrie, Uncle Tom Johnston, Uncle Jerry Cardin, etc. Looking back now it seems that it was disrespectful for a child of eight to address a fifty year old person by their first name, but at that time it seemed perfectly natural.

I remember sometime in the early 'forties Dad preaching at night with two Aladdin lamps hanging above the pulpit. They lighted the whole auditorium. I remember the windows all being open with no screens, moths and wasps flying around the lamps and a small baby crying on its pallet while the mother fanned it with a funeral home fan. Sometime in that decade electricity came to the community and we had electric lights.

During some of those years Dad was full time pastor at Morrilton, and would preach at Needs Creek on Saturday night or Sunday afternoon, and sometimes even on Saturday morning. One Saturday I remember after church we went to Uncle Tom Johnston's home for lunch. I don't know how many people were there, but a lot. When we got there, the ladies sent all the boys to catch chickens. We caught them and one of the ladies wrung their necks while other ladies heated water to clean them. While this was going on outside, other ladies were cooking vegetables, making desserts, biscuits and tea. They fried the chicken and served up a grand meal. The men ate first, the women second and all the kids last. I remember thinking that I would starve to death before our time came. I also remember thinking that all the chicken would be gone when it came time for us to eat, but the ladies had saved some back for us.

Another thing that impressed me at the church was the seating arrangements. There were three rows of pews, and as you faced the pulpit, the men sat on the left side, the women on the right and the young people and young couples sat in the center. When the service was over, the men would roll themselves a cigarette and smoke by the stove in the winter and outside in the summer. When the weather allowed, the men would all stay outside until the second song began before coming in.

The church was heated by two wood burning stoves, one on each side of the auditorium. For a time Dickie Mills and I were in charge of building the fires. We would meet early in the morning, carry in wood and kindling and build the fires. Then we would rush home to get dressed for church, then hurry back to make sure the stoves were warming the building. We were paid fifteen cents per fire, and the money came from the training service offering, if there was enough. Betty Williams collected the money and paid us.

In the winter, Thursdays were quilting time for the women in the church. They would bring pot luck lunches and have two quilting frames going at the same time. At the end of their day, they would roll up the quilt frames towards the ceiling where they would stay until the next Thursday. Quilting day was a wonderful day for all of us in school. We would jump off the bus at the church and race to the stoves where the leftover food would be. The women would make us stop and get a plate and act like we had some manners. School lunches left a lot to be desired, and we would be starved when we got to the leftovers at the church.

We didn't have any Sunday school rooms, so each class would occupy a section of the auditorium, usually only a couple of pews for each class. There would be a constant hum of conversation all during Sunday school. At the end of class, whoever was the song leader (the one I remember most was Fat Whitacre) would call for all singers to come to the choir. We would sing a couple of hymns, take the offering, then the sermon, the invitation and benediction. I remember that no one seemed to be in a hurry to leave when services were over. Today we are all in a hurry to get to the restaurant before the crowd gets there.

This is Christmas week, so naturally I thought about Cecil "Big Six" Glenn. At the Christmas program, we older boys would watch Cecil slip out of the church and come back in at the right time dressed as Santa Claus with candy and gifts for the little ones. I don't know where he got the "Big Six" handle.

I spent a lot of time with Sonny Loveless in the 'forties. Sometimes I would stay for a week with him, working in the fields, hoeing cotton, whatever there was to do. He and I spent as many hours as we could get away with in their pond. Fishing and swimming were our passions, and we spent many hours pursuing them. Their pond was also the baptizing hole used following the summer revival, the second Sunday in August. I remember thinking then that no one from Needs Creek could be saved any other time. I remember walking to church with the Loveless family in the summer, and Mrs. Clara would go barefooted to the big mulberry tree, sit down on the road bank, take a washcloth from her purse, clean her feet, put her shoes on and we would continue on to church. When I was staying with Sonny, every morning Mrs. Loveless would wake us up saying, "Shine, boys shine, like a watermelon on a pumpkin vine."

One time I spent a week with Bob Williams and he and Betty and I cleared a persimmon thicket so we could see their pond from the house. All we had to work with was a little hatchet, and Ted said that it looked like the beavers had been there. Another time Sonny and I went home with Bob from church, and we didn't have any play clothes. Gracie found us some. Sonny got a pair of overalls, and I had to wear a pair of Betty's jeans with the zippers on the sides. I made them swear they wouldn't tell anybody, but they told it at church that night. I was really embarrassed.

One time I was staying with Sonny, and the rest of the family were going to town. Sonny and I had our plans made, and the material gathered to build a diving board at the pond. Before they left, they issued lots of instructions. Don't get the gun out, clean up the kitchen after you eat lunch, don't do this, don't do that, don't leave the place. All the time they were telling us these things, we knew that the next one would be don't go to the pond. But it didn't come. By the time they got to Mr. Whitaker's, we were almost to the pond and stayed all day.

When we moved to the house we had built in '47, we set in to make garden and truck patches. We finished tearing down the canning kitchen, and cut the logs up for firewood. Then I started plowing up that area with the little garden tractor that Garland Abrams and Dad had built. I did pretty well except for one area where the plow would bounce out of the ground, and no matter how hard I tried, I couldn't plow it. The following Sunday, I told some of the men about it, and they laughed and said that was the basketball court. They would haul red clay and spread it out, put water on it, then walk on it to settle it down. They would then wait for it to dry then pull a sled with a scraper on it with two or three kids on it and scrape it down level. We had good crops on that area after we got Fat Whitaker to break the land with his big tractor. Thinking of Fat's tractor, a Farmall, I remember that the community was pretty well divided on the merits of tractors. John Deere and Farmall. Slim Day was a maverick I guess, he had an Allis Chalmers. He was also the first person I knew who plowed his cotton two directions.

Slim and Russell Mills owned a tree dog together, named Rock. He was a great tree dog and we used him many times squirrel hunting. One night at church in the summer he treed down on the creek. Dickie Mills and I didn't hear a word of the sermon, listening to old Rock. The minute the last amen was given, we took off to see what he had treed. It was a big tree and up in the top, we saw a cat, which we decided was a wild cat, so we got Russell and Dad to help us. They shot it and it lodged up in the tree, but they told us that it was only a house cat that had gone wild. We were really disappointed.

In the late forties all the farmers were engaged in an all out war with the boll weevils. Now anytime I smell something that smells like cotton poison my mind goes immediately to the church yard at Needs Creek in the summertime. It is a wonderful memory. Ted Williams bought a six-row "poisoner" that he put on his tractor. Bob and I spent several nights poisoning their cotton. We loved having to work at night when the dew was on.

I helped bale hay for Russell Mills and some others one whole summer. One time the rake brought up a load of hay and a big black snake came up out of the hay and Mr. John Parham grabbed it by the tail and popped it like a whip and popped its head off. I was really impressed. I also remember Mr. Parham getting mad at his Ford tractor and kicking it, breaking his foot. Thinking now, we called him and his wife Mr. and Mrs. instead of their first names.

One time we were hoeing cotton for Russell Mills in the Blackfork bottoms, in a bend of the creek where we couldn't get any fresh air, and we got out to the end of the rows and rested under a tree, when a little breeze came up. We were all wet with sweat, and the breeze felt so good that Uncle Jesse Mills said, "I'm coming down here Sunday and sit all day, this feels wonderful."

Homecoming was always a special time for the whole community. I guess I remember the food the most, spread on tables made of saw horses and old lumber with tablecloth covering. I get hungry now thinking of fresh peas and beans and tomatoes and okra, and fried chicken and chicken and dumplings and everything good that could be raised or gathered on the farm. Of course I remember the desserts like blackberry cobblers, and especially the hickory nut cake that Lois Nixon's mother would bring every year. They had a big hickory tree in their yard, and she would pick out enough nuts for her grand cake. How good it was!

I was six years old when the forties began and sixteen when they ended. In that decade we lived through a world war that affected everyone. The loss of young men devastated every community and Needs Creek was no exception. We saw the beginning of the nuclear age when terrible bombs were dropped in Japan, ending the war. We saw the men returning from the war and starting their lives over again. We saw the economy begin to grow after the depression and the war.

I believe my family was happier living at Needs Creek than anywhere we lived. Some of my fondest memories are there, in the summer gathering food from the garden, helping Mom can vegetables and working for others in the fields and meadows. I dreaded, "doing up the work," as Mother called it, in the winter, then coming in half frozen with a bucket of steaming milk and a few eggs, into a warm kitchen to the sights, sounds and smells of supper.

During that decade of the forties I heard, or learned, or absorbed the character traits that I most admire today. I may have heard them in Sunday school or in sermons, but I think I learned them mostly from my family and from the people of that community. Honesty, respect, responsibility, loyalty, reverence, manners, courtesy, thoughtfulness, patriotism, the work ethic, consideration of others, honor, integrity—these traits were the core of their lives. I think anyone living in the community who did not have these qualities in their lives would have been very uncomfortable living there, and there may have been some, but I didn't know them.

As I look back now at the age of seventy-five, I feel especially blessed that I could spend the formative years of my life connected to a place like Needs Creek. The quality and the character of the people had a profound effect on my life and I will always be grateful.

Dad and I dress out a hog.
Dad could really cure that meat

Dad and Grandfather Ward
in the 1930s at Bigelow

Dad loved to farm,
but never planted
so much it wasn't fun

Grandfather Richardson —
the other preacher in the
family — making a point

Dad baptizing in a creek
at the conclusion
of a revival

**I** was probably ten or eleven years old and had been hunting since I was five or six. I had graduated to a single barrel .410 gauge shotgun that I could handle pretty well. I hunted with Dad mostly, some with Grandpa and other members of the family, but that was about it. Dad was really tough on us about safety, and I guess it worked—at least none of us shot each other. I still don't know what prompted Dad to decide to take me on a really big hunt with men outside the family,

# Needs Creek Hunting

but he did. We were living at Morrilton at the time, so we got up before daylight and drove to Needs Creek to "Shep" Biggs' house. Someone else went with us that I think it was "Red" Day.

I don't have any idea how many coveys of quail we found that day but a lot of them. The men weren't so interested in shooting on the covey rise, though we did, as they were in the single shooting. They would take turns walking in on the point with someone else beside them in case more than one got up. Sometimes they let me take a turn, and I missed them all except the last time I shot. They said it was my turn, and I walked in. The bird got up, I shot and, wonder of wonders, it fell. I ran to it before the dogs could get there and picked it up, admired it, then put it in my game pouch—what a wonderful trophy! Looking back now, I'm sure one of the men killed it and let me claim it, but I sure didn't think of that then. They told what a fine shot it was and told me that it wouldn't be long before I would be getting my limit every day.

A lot of things made that day memorable for me. "Shep" knew where every covey of birds was and about how many birds were in each covey. Sometimes he would tell us to count the birds as they came up and not to shoot if there were less than eight. We had the whole community to hunt in. If any of the land was posted, I didn't know about it. At noon, we arrived at someone's house, and they invited us in to lunch. They may have known we were coming, but I don't think so. I don't remember anyone getting upset with the dogs that day. I wore a pair of new, sixteen-inch leather boots. We ate supper with "Shep" and Mildred, then went to church that night where Daddy preached. I went to sleep as soon as he started. We took about 50 dressed birds home that night.

It was probably an average sort of day for the men—plenty of birds, good exercise, good companionship, a Saturday well spent. But for a boy who had, for a day, been allowed to be a man, there was nothing ordinary about it. If it had been ordinary, I wouldn't have remembered it for 50 years.

Dad's bird dog, Pam, on point in the snow

T he adults were always talking, worrying about a war on the other side of the world. At age seven it didn't worry me until that Sunday when we were attacked. Even at that age I knew that something big and bad had happened. The prayers that night in church were different, more sincere, more humble, more earnest, more genuine sounding to a seven-year-old.

# World War II

I remember . . .

The tears, the fears, and the prayers as the men were being drafted and leaving. Throughout the war I never heard a public prayer that didn't include, "Bring our boys home safely."

The early years when defeats were constant and victories were few. The heroism of Jimmy Doolittle and his group taking off from carriers and bombing Japan, knowing that they didn't have enough fuel to get back and landing somewhere in China.

Saving pennies and buying savings stamps, putting them in the little book, and when it was full, trading it for a savings bond. The Burma-Shave sign that said, "Buying bonds means money lent, so they don't cost you one red cent."

Standing at the railroad tracks while a slow moving steam engine pulled a troop train through with a man in uniform at every window. Every one waved to me, and my arm got tired and I changed to the other. And Daddy said when I told him, "Never fail to wave at the soldiers no matter how tired you get."

The songs, "Lets remember Pearl Harbor as we go to victory," "Coming in on a wing and a prayer," "I'll be looking at the moon, but I'll be seeing you."

Our heroes—Ike, MacArthur, Nimintz, Rickenbacker, Marshall, Audie Murphy.

If you wanted a fight, call someone Hitler or Tojo and get ready.

In civics class when we had to have a current event to share, that couldn't be about the war, and how hard they were to find.

A truck convoy stopped on our street and the soldiers played marbles with us, and realizing many years later how homesick they were for their own little boys.

Rationing stamps and the sticker on the car windshield with a letter on the outside, and on the inside it said, "Is this trip really necessary?"

Helping my uncle put his car on blocks in the barn because he didn't have a stamp for a tire.

The magazine ads that said, "We're not making refrigerators now, we're making tanks. When we win the war we'll make refrigerators again."

The men coming home on leave sometimes just before they went overseas, and the happiness on their families' faces when they would arrive and the sadness when they would leave.

Then there were those who would never come home. I was with Dad in Morrilton one time and someone rushed up and said that a family in our church had received the dreaded telegram from the War Department that read, "We regret to inform you that your son has been killed in action." We went to the home and on the way, Dad said, "I already know the questions they will ask and I already know that I don't have any answers." In the next few days the blue star hanging in the front window was changed to a gold one and each time I looked at it I could hear the mother crying, "Why did my son have to die?" And no one knew the answer.

I remember when victory was declared in Europe. The fire truck drove all over town with the siren blaring and men sitting and standing all over it shooting guns in the air. I think every kid in town who had a bicycle rode in that parade. While in the Air Force I participated in a number of parades, one of them for then president Eisenhower, but no parade has ever equaled the parade we had on V.E. Day in Morrilton, Arkansas.

May we never take for granted the God given, blood bought freedom we enjoy in America today.

**P**eople built this barn. I am sure they felt good about their work. They had taken a spot of ground that covered 2,000 square feet and erected shelter for their livestock and the crops they would harvest. It was a good barn, built of the standard barn building materials, on a well-drained spot, and they were justifiably proud.

As soon as they left the day they finished it, nature began **Nature** to tear it down. Step by step, little by little, infinitely patient, so slowly that the human eye couldn't see it, She began to tear it down. The few drops of moisture that condensed on the underside of the metal roof that night did nothing but remove a few specks of oil that coated the metal. But it was a start. The blades of grass and weeds that the workmen had trampled as they worked began to straighten up that night and their roots grew a little, back towards the support posts where they could start the decaying process. The night breeze that blew on the metal roof didn't move the metal enough to see, but it created a little space under one of the lead head nails, so that moisture could get to the shank of the nail. A storm that came in the Fall didn't seem to bother the barn at all, and the men who built it were proud of their work. But the hailstones that hit the ground near the barn loosened the top soil just a bit so that the winter rains could wash it up against the base of the posts so that moisture would hold a little longer. Not much, but it was a start. In the winter when the ground froze and thawed, and froze and thawed, the support posts settled just a fraction of an inch. Not much, but it caused the nails to twist a little.

The men who built the barn knew that it would require maintenance. Periodically they tightened the nails that held the structure, and got up on the roof and tightened those nails. Each time this happened, Nature was set back a little but She never stopped working.

As the years went by the men finally sold the farm and moved to greener pastures. The man who bought it didn't farm it himself, he moved a tenant farmer in. The only thing this man was interested in was making as much money as he could, and though he recognized the quality in the barn, he didn't spend any time or money on it. Nature used this neglect to continue her work even more rapidly. The vines that grew around the posts climbed the posts, providing a place where rainwater could collect and soak into the wood. As the vines grew stronger they began to push up on the tin roof and force the now loosened nails to give way. A strong springtime storm blew through and blew the roof away in a few places, allowing more rainwater to soak into the rafters and the rest of the support structure.

Nature has completed her work. No trace of the barn can be seen. I first saw the barn more than 50 years ago, and it was 30 years old at that time. With her job on the barn complete, She can now concentrate on the new structures that we are building. It may take her longer to take these down, but She is very patient.

Barn at old house

Once again he was ten years old, hoeing the cotton, and for the last hour of the long, hot morning listening for the dog horn that his mother used to call them in for dinner. His plans all made, at the first sound from the horn he dropped his hoe, and raced for the house. He knew his mother would let him have a cold biscuit and piece of sausage, and he grabbed it and raced away, his bare feet ignoring the rocks and stickers, to spend his dinner hour at his own special, secret place.

# Nidy Hole

As he drew near, he stopped running and quietly slipped to the back of the 20-foot high bluff, climbed to the flat top, and lay still, watching. There was so much to see in the 30-foot-long and 20-foot-wide hole of water that was four feet deep in places. Out in the middle were three large rocks where he often saw the little perch that he would catch later. The things he had seen since he first discovered his place! A red fox slipping up and getting a drink of water—a mother 'coon teaching her three babies how to fish for their meal—a big snake swallowing a frog, something he told his sisters about so they would stay away—a lizard sunning itself on a rock and a hawk swooping down and grabbing it. Sometimes after he had finished eating and watching, he would climb down and go to the shallow end, take off his clothes and wade or swim, climb back out and sit on a rock and let the sun and wind dry him off, get dressed, then see what tracks he could find around the edge of the water.

That day that he had caught his first fish all by himself, and the time he killed his first squirrel with his little rifle, he could almost feel again the excitement he had felt on those days. The time he was there and a severe storm came suddenly, and he got up under the bluff, and was looking at a large oak tree when it was struck by lightning. It was scary, but he felt secure under his bluff.

His boyhood was more than half a century behind him now, but the memories were as clear as though it was happening today.

Dad fishing in the Nidy Hole.
The place was a significant place in his memory and remains so in ours

photograph by John Ward

**W**hen I think of Mother, my mental picture of her is not when she is dressed up to go somewhere, though she did that a lot. It isn't a picture of her in church, though she was there three or four times a week all her life. I never see her in bed, though she spent a third of her life there. Sometimes I see her sitting, but not very often. Occasionally in my pictures she is sad or serious looking, and I wonder what is wrong. The picture that

# My Mother

is permanently engraved on my mind is a picture of her wearing an apron, her face with a wide smile and her teeth showing, and her hands moving, illustrating whatever it is she is telling.

I think that she was the most positive minded person I ever knew. I never remember her looking at the bad side of anything. No matter how bad it was, there was somehow always a good side. Not only things, but people as well. I know that I did things that she didn't approve of or was disappointed in but I guess she chose to ignore them and look for something good to talk about. She used positive reinforcement long before the phrase became popular. By letting me hear her tell someone else how I did up the work, or plowed the garden or whatever, she made me want to do even better, though my resolve to do better sometimes got lost in the shuffle.

I suppose that finances were a constant problem for them as they are for all of us. One time when I was old enough to know they were upset, they applied for a loan to re-finance the house and consolidate their bills, and the loan company came and turned down the loan because they didn't have enough land with the house. Dad was devastated, but Mom said that there would be a way.

When she talked about people I don't ever remember her running anyone down. When we would criticize someone she would tell us that there were probably things we didn't know about that caused them to act the way they did. As we were married and brought our spouses to her home we learned right away that they were family just as much as we were, and never be critical in her presence.

One thing that stands out in my mind was her boundless energy. She never seemed to tire, though I know she did. She would be up in the mornings before anyone else, working in the garden, or putting out two or three loads of washing.

Then she would go to the kitchen when it was time for everyone else to get up and prepare a big breakfast. She was convinced that it was the most important meal of the day. Her biscuits, made thousands of times, were always the same, always plenty of them, and made without a recipe except for what was in her head. I think she made them mostly by feel. I believe that the two places she was happiest were the kitchen and the garden.

Most of the meals she prepared were plain basic meals with a lot of vegetables, but sometimes when she had a reason to she could fancy them up too. One of her favorite things to make was individual salads made on a lettuce leaf with pear halves, shredded cheese with a dollop of mayonnaise and a red cherry on top. At Christmas time she would make red and green divinity candy and guard it against a houseful of kids.

If I were objective I guess I would say that she was always overweight, but it didn't seem that way at all. She was always just right.

I don't ever remember her telling me that she loved me, but I never doubted it. She was not very demonstrative, but she didn't need to be.

I guess most ladies in that time wore aprons, but mother was almost undressed without one. She had everyday aprons and Sunday aprons, and almost always had one on. In almost all my mental pictures of her she has an apron on.

In the mental picture that I have of her in the winter, she is wearing some of Dad's old khaki pants under her dress, an old red checkered coat and a scarf on her head. Another wintertime picture is her coming in from doing up the work, backing up to the fire and pulling her dress up to warm her legs. When she would turn around the backs of her legs would be almost blistered.

I guess she taught us manners negatively. It is ill mannered to do this or that. It is ill mannered to take the last piece of anything. When called, answer with "Ma'am" or "Sir," never with "What."

I never remember her getting down on her knees to do anything. She could bend to the ground to grabble potatoes, then put them in her apron pocket—along with an egg, or a few beans or peas, some seeds she planned to plant, or maybe a fishing cork with a line and hook carefully wound up.

I know she was always interested in our education, but in retrospect it would be hard to see. I never once remember her asking me if I had my homework, how I was doing in school, or what kind of grades I was making. She somehow got across the idea that she trusted me to study and make good grades and that it was up to me. I wondered sometimes why she wasn't involved with the P.T.A. and my school programs, and many years later realizing that she was a pastor's wife with eight kids and not much time for anything else. She wasn't there when I sang a solo at my sixth grade graduation, but I didn't expect her and didn't think anything about it. When I was in the eleventh grade at Quitman she rode the school bus to see me in the class play and the other kids wondered why I was so excited.

She liked nothing better than fishing, even when the catch was small

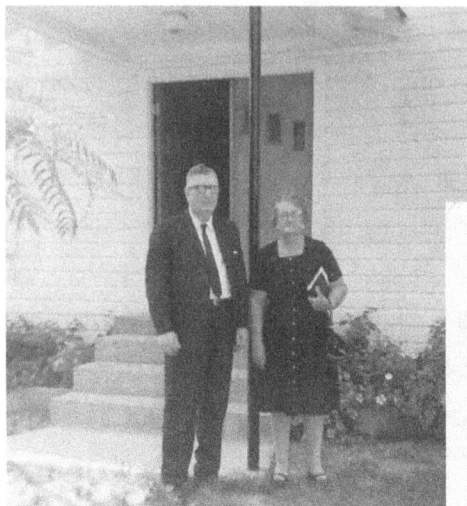

Dad and mother
in front of Old Euseba Church

Dad and mother,
probably before they married

Mom with her little calf. She was so proud, as were we all

**H**er hands didn't have long, graceful fingers with painted fingernails. In fact, I never remember her nails being painted. Her fingers were short and her hands small. I remember them being just right.

I remember those hands giving each of us a Carter's Little Liver Pill at night when we lived in Mississippi—when she believed # My Mother's Hands
that was what we needed to purify our blood. I also can see them pulling a limber switch from a tree for disciplinary purposes.

I see them in the kitchen, one of her favorite places, making biscuits every morning. She would fill a big, wooden bowl with flour, make a hole in the middle, then add shortening, baking powder, salt or whatever—measuring everything with those stubby fingers—adding buttermilk, mixing all this in the bowl and making perfect biscuits every morning for 50 years.

I see her hands holding a bowl of butter, fresh from the churn, squeezing, turning, adding salt, working all the water out of it, dipping the butter mold into hot water, filling it with butter then turning it out on a saucer. Then I see them opening a biscuit, slicing a big slice of this butter, putting it in the biscuit, letting it melt a little, opening it up again, adding a big spoonful of muscadine jelly and eating it.

I see them shelling peas into her apron, her thumbnails purple-stained, then picking up the corners of her apron and pouring the peas into a pan for washing and inspecting. I see her using one hand to measure salt to season the peas she was cooking. I guess she had some official measuring spoons, and probably used them sometimes, but I only remember her using her hands.

I see her hands grabbling new potatoes with a fork, very carefully scratching the dirt away so she wouldn't damage the other potatoes in the hill. Then she would pick and shell enough English peas to prepare a grand vegetable dish.

When she would cook fried potatoes, she would peel and slice the potatoes into a bowl of water, get the grease hot, add the potatoes a handful at a time, cover the skillet with a lid, then turn and mash the potatoes with a spatula.

Some would be brown and some not, but they would all be tender and good.

Her favorite meat was cured ham. I can see her grasping a ham hanging in the smokehouse or on the back porch in her left hand, then taking the old red-handled butcher knife and cutting the ham to the bone. Then she would cut down two or three inches and back out—getting a chunk about three by six inches. She would take that to the stove, slice it into the skillet, hot with bacon drippings, and cook it. When she had taken out the ham, she would pour the juice from the skillet into a bowl, add some water to the skillet and pour it into the bowl to make wonderful brown gravy.

I see those hands at garden-planting time, taking seeds from her apron pocket and dropping them two at a time—eight inches apart—as though they wouldn't grow any other way.

I see them so many times carefully threading a worm on a fishhook for herself or one of the children or grandchildren down at the pond.

I see them in the heat of summer at Morrilton fixing herself a bowl of ice cubes and placing it near the ironing board to eat while ironing, trying to stay cool.

I see her hands pause from cooking to tell something—she needed them to talk. She would hold them palms up to keep from dripping whatever she had on her hands as their motions punctuated her story.

I see one of them taking her glasses off, picking up the tail of her apron with the other one and cleaning her glasses.

I see those hands with a brush and paints creating a work of art for each of us; a talent we discovered accidentally.

In all my memories of her hands, they are always moving.

And then she died, and her hands were still . . . and maybe that was the first time I had seen them that way.

I don't know when my first memories of Grandpa occurred. I remember him and Grandma coming to Laurel, Mississippi, and we all went to the Gulf, so I wasn't more than five or six. I remember going to Bigelow when they lived in a little sharecropper house near Uncle Ernest, Grandma and Aunt Colon plucking the geese for their feathers and Jimmy Charles getting pecked on the head by a

# Memories and Lessons from Grandpa Ward

blue jay when he climbed up a tree to see their nest. I remember Jimmy Charles, John, Bob and me taking a carbide lamp and using it to write our names on the walls of the barn and smokehouse (there were no fire marshals at that time).

One time I went to see them when they lived in a little house in Bigelow beside the Catholic Church, and Grandpa took me squirrel hunting. We walked from the house to a creek, and, on the way, we met an old, black man whose clothes were crusted with salt from sweating. When we were far enough away that he wouldn't hear me, I mentioned that he was really dirty. Grandpa stopped and looked directly at me and said, "Boy, clothes that are dirty from hard work are the finest a man can wear."

We were still-hunting, sitting quietly and watching for squirrels, and we stayed until dark. Just before we were ready to leave, two owls started hooting at each other very near us. They weren't hooting exactly but talking to each other in owl-talk, and it was really scary. I looked at Grandpa for reassurance, and he gave me a look that said, "I don't know what that is." Then I really got scared until he grinned. On the way back, we hitched a ride with a man in a wagon, we sat in the back end of the wagon and when we got to the house we just stepped off, waved a "thank you" to the farmer and went up the drive to the house.

I spent more time with them when they lived at Damascus than anywhere else. They lived on the Carrell place in the main part of the house, and we built our house as an addition to theirs. I stayed with them a lot before we moved there. In the spring, Grandpa would be plowing, breaking up the land with old Joe and Mandy, the mules that were his pride and joy, and I would be sent by Grandma to take him a fresh drink of water. I remember walking in the furrow barefooted, and I loved the feel of the dirt on my feet and the smell of the fresh, plowed earth.

I remember him shocking me to my toes one time when I took him a drink. He took the bucket and said, "Boy, you got piss ants in it." At the age I was then, that was real cussing. Sometimes I would go to the fields at almost dinnertime, and when he unhooked the team, he would let me ride old Joe back to the house.

He took me fishing one time down on Pine Mountain Creek. I don't remember whether we caught anything or not, but I found some ripe huckleberries, showed them to him, we picked them—or rather pulled them—ripe, red and green, put them into his fishing pouch and Grandma made a little pie.

One time he took me hunting down towards the creek. I don't know how old I was, but old enough to carry a gun. We were crossing a fence in a neighbor's pasture, I knocked a staple from a fence post and the wire came loose. I hooked the wire on top of the post and Grandpa said, "I'll wait here while you go back to the house and get a hammer and staple and fix that fence." I tried to talk him out of it, saying that I could maybe find something to fix it with, but he just pointed towards the house. I thought at the time that it was at least a mile, but, looking back now, it was probably less than a quarter of that. I brought the hammer and the staple and fixed the fence, then he told me to take the hammer back. Then I really tried to argue, but he just pointed towards the house. When I finally got back and we were going on hunting, he said that he could have fixed that fence, but he wanted me to learn that somebody else's property is sacred, and you don't mess it up.

One time he let me take Spot, his Feist squirrel dog, and my .22 rifle hunting by myself. It was the greatest hunt I had ever had. Spot treed five squirrels, I found four of them and killed them. I shot three of them in the head and one in the neck, and, when Grandpa and I skinned them that afternoon, all he said was that I ruined a good piece of meat on the one where I missed the head. I was really disappointed that he didn't brag on me until the next day Grandma sent me to the store for something. I overheard Grandpa talking to some other men around the stove, and he was really bragging on me.

One time after we had moved into the part of the house we had added on and after Mandy had been killed at the sorghum mill and Daddy had bought a horse named Shorty to work with old Joe, we spent an evening shelling corn to take to the mill the next day. The adults would "nub" all the bad grains off, then give the ears to us and we would shell them. We shelled a tow sack full that night, and, the next morning, Grandpa said he wanted me to take the corn to the mill. He caught old Shorty, put a bridle on him, put the sack of grain on his back, then helped me up behind the sack and sent me off. When I got to the mill, the operator unloaded the corn and me, then proceeded to grind the corn into meal. When he finished, he got a scoop and got three or four scoops out of our meal. He loaded the rest of the meal and me on the horse. I would have made Shorty run all the way home, but I was afraid I would fall off. I had to get to Grandpa quick and tell him that the man had stolen some of our meal. When I finally got there and told Grandpa, he just laughed and told me that the man had taken his toll. I asked him what a toll was, and he said that it was our way of paying the man for grinding our corn.

One time we were fishing somewhere, I got bored I guess and wandered off. I found a rock about four inches square sticking out of the ground. I pushed and pulled and finally got it out and took it to show Grandpa. He looked at it, asked where I got it and said to take it back. We took it back, he put it in the hole and packed the dirt back around it. He then pulled a limb from a tree, hit me a couple times—which didn't hurt—then told me that the rock was a land corner, that people had been killed over land corners and that I was never to bother them. To the best of my knowledge I have never touched one since.

One of my best memories was a time in the fall when Grandpa was making sorghum down at the spring, and I helped him cook off the last batch of syrup. Everyone else had gone but the two of us. The fire had burned down to coals, and I remember the two lanterns hanging from the posts near the end of the pan which gave enough light for me to see to get water from the spring to pour into the upper end of the pan. As he would work the syrup down from a section, I would have to quickly fill that section with water so the pan wouldn't burn. When we finished, he blew out one of the lanterns, picked up a bucket of the hot syrup, I carried the other lantern and we walked to the house up the lane. It was late

September, about ten o'clock and almost cold. I remember the full moon and the smell of fall as we walked to the house. Mother saw the lantern moving up the lane, put a pan of biscuits in the oven and when we got there, they were brown. I cut some of them open, cut off a big slice of home-churned butter, put it in the biscuits, poured the hot syrup over them, watched the butter melt and had a wonderful meal.

It seemed to me, as a child, that Grandpa cared more for his mules than just about anything. When he came in from working them all morning, he put them in the barn lot so they could get a drink and roll, then he would feed them. Sometimes I got to help him, and he would tell me each time, "Give old Joe ten ears of corn and Mandy nine," because she was smaller. I would shuck the corn and put it in their stalls, and he would bring them in to eat. All this was done before we would go to the house to eat. When he would hook them to the wagon to go to town or somewhere, he would brush them until they shined. When Mandy got excited, ran into the lead pole at the sorghum mill and got killed, I remember him in the barn lot that night for a long time trying to comfort old Joe who had lost his lifetime work-mate.

One time I was with Grandpa and Grandma at the Carrell place in Damascus, and, in the night, it snowed about two or three inches. Grandpa and I were going rabbit hunting, but he said that before we went, he had to sow his lespedeza seed. He explained, as I walked behind him and as he cranked the handle on the sower, that by sowing on the snow, he could tell exactly where the seeds were going, and they would sink into the wet ground as the snow melted. Makes perfect sense.

We—Grandpa, Dad, John, Bob and me—went turkey hunting one time over towards Cedar Creek, and we camped where Bread Creek runs into Alum Fork. We got there in the early afternoon and set up camp then started catching little perch for bait for a throw line in the big hole in alum Fork. We caught a lot more little fish than we needed for bait, so Grandpa cooked the rest of them for supper that night. They were small, he fried them whole, and really brown, and we ate them—bones and all. Wonderful meal! Grandpa made coffee late that afternoon in a big pot that was blue speckled enamel. He filled it about two-thirds full of water, got that boiling good, dumped the coffee in, put the lid on and moved it off the fire. A few minutes later, he added a cup of cold water to settle the grounds, and they let us all drink some with Pet milk in it. I've liked coffee since then.

Tony and Joey on a hunt with Pawpaw

These girls really kicked off the gospel music tours for the family.
Loweta is at left, and Marketa is with her accordion, with two good friends

The family posed after a recording session. Suzy is at the piano

Me, Ronnie Evans and Bill. A pause during one of the rehearsals

Rehearsing in the recording studio for one of the Ward Family albums

The group on stage. Just about everybody made it to every concert

The boys formed a trio and performed at many of the concerts

**I** think that I should probably call it the hunting horn, but all my life it has been called Grandpa Ward's dog horn. I don't know when Dad got it from Grandpa, but it is one of the first things that I can remember us having that had anything to do with hunting. We always had at least one hound, and anytime Dad took the dog hunting, he carried the horn. It was as much a

# The Dog Horn

part of the hunt as the five-cell flashlight that he also carried and in later years the .22 pistol.

The horn was made from a pretty large bull or steer, and I never heard who made it or when. As I examine it now, I'm convinced that it was extremely well made. Many of the horns that I see are made with a wooden mouthpiece, but this one is made of horn, and the mouthpiece was perfectly fitted to the horn and then glued in place. I don't remember any of our hounds coming when he blew the horn, but they probably did. I think that it was a way for Dad to re-connect to his childhood and to Grandpa.

Dad told many times about when Grandpa wanted to go night hunting with some of his buddies, he would go out on the back porch about dark and blow the horn. There was probably some sort of signal, like a certain number of blows, then he would wait for an answer. Kennedy, Tipton, Edwards, I don't know all the names, but they would answer with their own horns. If they wanted to go hunting, they would all meet in the middle and bring their dogs. Sometimes Dad said they would run their dogs all night after a fox. As I've thought about those times he told about, I don't remember Dad ever talking about going with them. He went always when it was a daytime hunt, and he went many times at night when it was just him and Grandpa, but not with Grandpa and his buddies.

As I think about Grandfather's life, I think about what a hard life it was. Out of an uncomfortable bed before daylight, build a fire for cooking, feed the mules, get the kids all up and off to school or to the fields, plowing the poor land, coming in at noon for a lunch of food he had raised, resting the team for an hour, back to the fields and work until dark, eat supper, sit for a while, then go to bed to get up the next morning and start it all over again. If rain kept them from the fields, they cut wood with a crosscut saw, split it with an axe and wedge, hauled it to the house and stacked it. The physical part of his life was hard enough, but I think the mental part was just as hard. The awesome responsibilities of feeding and caring for a family of ten, constant fears of crop failures, the health of his family as well as the health of his animals, fires and storms, it was enough to weigh anyone down with worry.

He was involved with the church and the community, and had social contact there, but I think that sometimes, like the rest of us, he just wanted to get away. Away from responsibilities, the daily work routine, just get away. It was at these times that I think that he would go out on the back porch with the horn and call up his buddies. Since his hunting buddies were living basically the same kind of life that he was, they were probably ready for some time away as well, and would usually answer the call. I wish I had a tape recording of their conversation around the fire. I'm sure they talked about their crops, how much they would get for their bale of cotton, their conversation interrupted by the baying of the hounds, then the talk would shift to which dog was leading the pack, whether it was a gray or red fox they were chasing.

Perhaps it was a time when they could talk, man to man, in a way they couldn't talk at home.

"I can't understand that boy of mine. He's 15 years old and thinks he knows as much as I do!"

"I know what you mean, mine's already talking about when he gets 18, he's gonna join the Army! How stupid can you get?"

"What if you had a house full of girls that didn't think of nothin' but boys and clothes? One of them got hold of a catalog full of clothes, and you'd think they found a gold mine! They can't even hoe corn without leaning on their hoe handle and talking about them clothes."

"Well, boys, we're living in a different world, you know. The way people in Washington are talking, we're gonna be in a war 'fore long. They're saying that if we don't go help them people in Europe, that them Germans will take over the world."

"I think them people over there oughta take care of their own problems, and leave us alone. We got enough problems just feeding our families, we can't worry about them people on the other side of the ocean."

"John, you read that newspaper, what are they saying?"

"Boys, they are saying that if that Kaiser over there takes over Europe, that the next thing he wants is the rest of the world, and that's us."

"Well, I think that our granddads came over here and made a country, then had to fight them Europeans as you call them just to keep it, then I think they oughta fight their own fights just like we did."

"I know what you mean, and I pretty well agree with you, but it is a different world we're living in. Also, they're saying that this will be the war to end all wars. That would be a pretty good thing, too."

"Well, boys, we can't fix all these problems tonight, and I gotta git the middles plowed out of the corn or I'll have more to worry about next winter. Besides, I think our dogs are about played out anyway."

"Yeah, I'm gonna see if I can call Roy and Singer off the trail, and I'll see you boys next time."

I'm sure that the horn sounds today just like it sounded 90 years ago when Grandpa called Roy and Singer off the trail. I wonder if these hills remember the sound?

I talked today to a man who was looking for his dogs that had been running last night. He was using a device with an antenna on it trying to home in on an electronic attachment on the dog's collar. I couldn't help but wonder if his dogs would come to a dog horn. Or if he even had one.

As I sit here in the cabin today, I look at the horn hanging beside the fireplace near the painting of Old House, I can almost see Grandfather standing on the back porch blowing the horn and listening for the horns of his buddies. I think I can hear the horn.

Grandfather and
Grandmother Ward
and their children
at the time.
That's Dad on
Grandfather's left
shoulder

Grandfather and
Grandmother
Ward with their
girls and Dad

**G**randfather John Thomas Ward was at one time the church clerk and song leader of the Euseba Baptist Church on Black Hill Road. Dad often talked about how he would introduce a new song. He would strike his tuning fork on the pulpit or on his head, get the pitch, then sing the song. He would then give the pitch and the congregation would sing with

# O Come Angel Band

him. One of his favorite songs was "O Come, Angel Band" and he would sing it often.

When he lay dying at Old House in 1951, he had been in a coma for two days and Uncle Carl was sitting with him. Uncle Carl told me that Grandfather awakened from the coma and said in a clear voice, "Come, Angel Band," closed his eyes and died.

My latest sun is sinking fast,
My race is nearly run.
My strongest trials now are past,
My triumph is begun.

O come, angel band, come and around me stand,
O bear me away on your snowy wings,
To my immortal home.
O bear me away on your snowy wings,
To my immortal home.

Grandmother Ward is dying. The daughters are gathered around the bed

A flag was important to me and we put this one on a permanent pole up high for all to see

John is holding a tape measure but Joe is eyeballing only whatever is going to be cut

The place of my dreams with the first snow on it

Me and Dena kicked back after serving up another incredible meal at the cabin. I was tired but happy

The Bee Branch Post Office is falling down. Not the current post office on Highway 92, but the one on Ivywood Road that gave the town its name. We call this one simply Old House. My grandfather, John Ward, bought the farm and Old House in about 1909 or 1910. My father Roy Ward was then eight years old, having been born in 1902 in a house across Bee Branch from Old House. Some of his younger siblings were born in Old House, and some of his older siblings were married there.

# The Naming of Bee Branch

They lived there until about 1918, when the lure of cotton that grew "as tall as a man" took them to "the bottoms" and England, Arkansas, where my father was married and entered the ministry.

His ministry took us to a number of places. I was living in my ninth home when I got married and left home. As a result of this moving from place to place, we never had a place that we really called home. Dad felt like the Johnson Place was home to him, so we children adopted it as our home also. Dad bought the farm in 1950 from Archie Tipton, and we lived there for about a year. He sold it a few years later and they moved to another pastorate.

In 1969 a friend of mine bought the place and I agreed to take care of it. For the next fifteen years it was our weekend camping place, a place to take friends, a place for family homecomings, and a place for the family to establish the Ward Family Christmas, a tradition.

William Brown, in his History of Damascus, says "Mail service was quite a problem for the early settlers for several years. As families moved in, at first there was no post office nearby. Some would have their mail sent to Martinville and some to Bee Branch, which was then located in what is now known as the Fairbanks community, on a big branch where many honey bees gathered for water. Thus the origin of the name of the post office on Highway 65, north of Damascus, Bee Branch." Fairbanks is about a mile and a half northeast of Old House.

Estella Johnson Clayton, in her history of Greasy Valley and Bee Branch, written in 1935, says "Many people, especially non-residents, wonder why Bee Branch has such a queer name. A short time previous, or during the Civil War, a post office was established on what is known in this section as Negro Hill, near the bank of a stream that was and still is called Bee Branch. From all reports, handed down from the days of the early settlers, this valley was noted for its many bees and fat bears. There seems to have been a larger colony of bees on this particular stream than anywhere else in this section, so being original people, they gave original names. When the post office was moved to what is known locally as the Billy Lankford old place, near where Roscoe Summers now lives, it still retained the name of Bee Branch. Just prior to 1879, the post office was moved from the Lankford old place to another log building in Crossroads, the original name of the present town of Bee Branch."

According to documents received from the Post Office Department in Washington, the post office was located in the NE Quarter of Section 7, Township 9, Range 12 W in Van Buren County, Arkansas.

I have been told all my life that Old House was the original Bee Branch post office, and my father told me that the front door with a mail slot in it was removed and used in another house on the hill south of the house. Bee Branch, the stream, is made up from springs on the old farm, and is the only stream so named in the county. It runs into the North Cadron just below the Ral Thompson Ford.

Old House has now completed its life. It was built of hewed logs in about 1850 by William Johnson. My grandfather added the kitchen, dog trot, and the "ell" room in 1910. My father added a room and bath on the back in 1950. It has been repaired and re-modeled a number of times, but nature has won. It has seen births and deaths, sadness and happiness, good crops and crop failures. It has sent the children born under its roof out into the world to make their contribution. It has made its contribution to Arkansas, to Van Buren County, and to my family. Good-by, Old House.

**A**unt Don bloomed today. That's not her real name of course, her name is Lula Elmus Ward Tipton. She is a purple iris that Aunt Don planted in about 1918 at the house where Howard was born. The house was at the top of the hill north of Old House. Part of the house was still there in 1950 when we lived at Old House. Judy, Bill and I used a part of the remainder of the

# Aunt Don Bloomed Today

house as shelter and a place to play mumble de peg, while waiting for the school bus. Aunt Don now grows in my flower garden.

The irises she planted in her front yard were probably a gift from a neighbor. Maybe they were a wedding gift. They have survived for about 85 years with little or no care. They have survived severe droughts, fires, and floods. They are survivors. And what I've said about these flowers I can say about my ancestors. I try to compare the way I live with the way they lived. What would Aunt Don have thought if she could have walked into her little house and flipped a switch and the room would light up? What if she could have walked to the sink and turned on running water? What about hot running water? If she could have walked to the refrigerator, got a glass of ice and poured a Coke over it? How about adjusting the temperature of the house with a thermostat? Any of these events which we consider basic necessities would have been undreamed of luxuries to her. She lit up her house with a coal oil lamp. She drew her water from a well or carried it from a spring. If she wanted hot water, she built a fire in the stove or the fireplace, put the water in a kettle and heated it. Her refrigerator was either the spring or the well house where she would draw fresh water several times a day and pour it into a tub with her milk and other things in it. Her house was cooled in the summer by whatever wind happened to blow. In the winter the amount of heat in the house depended on the size of the fire she had built.

She, along with the rest of our ancestors, were survivors. They did what they had to do when it had to be done.

Jimmy Charles Brown so eloquently put it this way in a letter about "The Spirit of Old House." He says, "The stories often remind me of the great stock from which we descended, and provide for me a pillar of strength that I can reach back and touch."

Enough said.

Aunt Don, always with coffee and dressed to the Nines

T hree years ago, I bought and planted my first roses. The first I had planted in a number of years. I bought a book, "The New Rose Expert," and read it carefully. With equal care, I selected the roses I wanted, "Mr. Lincoln" being the first one I wanted because it had been my Mother's favorite. I prepared the bed with some advice from my local rose expert, Paula Adlong.

# The Ultimate Chemical Spray for Roses

I planted 15 that first year, and by year's end had culled five or six of them, relegating them to another bed. The rest of them did pretty well that year, and the next year I added several more, being more selective this time. I said that I read my book carefully, but I really didn't carefully read the uninteresting chapter on diseases and insects. I learned a lot from actual experience. I sprayed bugs, hosed them off, sprayed again and again, waging continual war. I actually had a pretty good year last year, having enough to share with friends, and almost always a fresh bud each morning to provide a "Morning Rose" for my spouse.

This year was to be a great one. I had carefully pruned and mulched, fertilized early, always watching for any signs of diseases or bugs. I had some aphids early, and a few other bugs, and handled them with my sprayer.

Then I discovered the ultimate chemical. Accidentally. I noticed bugs and sprayed again. With this ultimate weapon I eliminated black spot, aphids, mildew, sawfly, rose stem girdler, spider mites, rust, purple spot and dieback. With one spraying. It is called Roundup and is available from your local store. I don't know that it actually killed all the insects, but it killed twenty-six of my roses and three of my sister's roses and didn't leave anything for the insects to eat, so I guess they died of starvation.

Although I haven't replaced all my roses yet, I have replaced about half of them. I also spent a dollar and thirty-nine cents for a felt tip pen and have labeled my sprayers.

Such a sad occasion when Paul Marsh, Joey's very best friend, died suddenly. We erected a tree and created a plaque in his honor

Their friendship began nine years ago. In that nine years they hunted, fished, and worked together anytime they had time off from their jobs. What one of them had to do—moving, painting, work on their houses, work up here on the family farm—they did it together. They spent a week in Florida working on Paul's dad's home, they went to Arizona to move Tori's dad's things

# Joey and Paul

after he passed away. But they were passionate about anything outdoors. Hunting and fishing, four-wheeling, cutting wood, cleaning fencerows, building deer stands, building and setting up deer feeders, anything outside, that was their place. They were especially excited when Dena and I bought the ten acres from Jenifer with plans to build a cabin. They came to help any time they could get away. I found Paul's name in my journal more than a hundred times in the last five years. The foundation, insulation, framing, painting, roof, every part of the cabin they were involved in it. They built and Paul brought up the deer feeder that has given all of us so much pleasure. Paul brought his daughter to hunt with him when she was only four or five, brought his nephew to deer hunt, always thinking of others.

This friendship was something rare and special from its beginning, and it made such an impression on the rest of us that any time it was mentioned, anyone who knew both of them would comment on it. Someone has said that if you count your friends on your fingers and it takes more than one hand, you are probably fooling yourself. Another said, "One friend in a lifetime is much; two are many; and three are hardly possible." Joey had many friends down through the years, but none of them were ever as close as he and Paul. Someone has described true friendship this way: If you were arrested in a foreign country and could only make one phone call, this would be the one you would call. That is the way it was for them.

This remarkable friendship ended in November, 2008. Paul called Joey the night before opening day of deer season from their camp. They were members of the Tall Pines Hunting Club in south Arkansas near Camden where they had a lease on about a thousand acres of land. Joey was at our home with the family that night, and Paul encouraged him to get to camp as soon as he could. He had to drop off some paperwork at his office the next morning and didn't get to the camp until six in the morning. Some of the other men in the camp called Joey just before he got there and told him they thought something was wrong with Paul, but he thought they were just pulling a prank. He got to the trailer and found Paul, who had died sometime in the night. He called the sheriff who brought the medical examiner, then called his wife and sent her to Tori, Paul's wife, then he called Tori and broke the news to her. Paul had a complete physical two weeks before, and only got the results from his heart tests on Tuesday before he died on Friday. All the tests indicated that his health was good. He died from a heart attack. He was 43 years old.

Although I am saddened so deeply for Joey, I don't think that I have ever been so proud of him. He took charge at the camp, then went to the funeral home with Tori and helped make all the arrangements. The funeral home was standing room only for the funeral, and Paul and Joey and the other pall bearers were dressed in camouflage clothing.

Joey gathered up Paul's guns and equipment and came home that Saturday afternoon. We went to his house and he and I embraced and cried for a long time, Joey sobbing deep, heartbroken sobs. On Monday, he came up here and sat on Paul's deer stand all day, grieving, trying to get back something rare and precious he had lost.

I think that most difficult part of parenting is seeing your children hurting and not being able to fix it. When they are very small, sometimes a band-aid on a scratch is sufficient, but band-aids don't work on hurts like this.

John, Bill, and I wanted to plant a tree in Paul's memory, and Joey and Tori agreed. Joey and I met at the nursery and he looked at a lot of trees before he decided on a red maple called October Blaze. I bought it and he brought it up here that weekend. I prepared a hole and John and Bill came and helped us plant it. Joey called and said that the people at Virco were making a plaque to put near the tree. Their friend Melinda designed it and they cast it in heavy aluminum. It says, "In loving memory of Paul Marsh, 1965-2008. For everything there is a season. Ecclesiastes." Joey brought it to me and I cast it in concrete and placed it in front of the tree. On Saturday, February 7, 2009, thirteen of us met at the cabin for breakfast and formally dedicated it. It was an emotional moment for all of us, but especially for Joey and Tori.

We placed the tree near the road on the East side of the cabin where it can easily be seen and I'm already looking forward to next October.

I really jumped into farming with this old Ford tractor

R ed was a 'coon hound, a red tick, one of the best breeds around. He was a hunting dog, and all he had ever dreamed of being was the best 'coon dog around. The possibility that he would be anything else never entered his mind. If you were a 'coon dog, you chased 'coons. Period. Then he had been adopted by a couple. They were wonderful people and he loved them dearly. They were not at all interested in his

# Red's Last Run

talents chasing 'coons, only in himself. They had fed, groomed, doctored, and cared for him as though he was a member of the family, and after a number of years, he finally gave up the idea of being a champion 'coon dog, content to live out the rest of his life as a revered family pet.

He hadn't felt good for the last few weeks, nothing particular wrong, he just hadn't felt good. He was more tired than usual, and had lost interest in chasing cars or other dogs. What he really enjoyed now was lying in the back yard in the November sun and sleeping. When he slept, he often dreamed. Mostly dreams of his youth. "The Chase—Ah! The Chase!" In his dreams he was once more running with the pack. Old Drum, the leader, Belle, Blue, and the rest of them. It was always a damp night after it had been cold for a few days with all the 'coons stirring and the smell of them lying near the damp ground. In his dreams he was always at or near the head of the pack, partly because of his speed, but mostly because he was smarter than the others. Old Drum often said that Red could think like a 'coon.

When he awakened from one of these dreams, he often wondered why the dreams were always about his youth. Those had been wonderful, exciting times for sure.

He was restless tonight, probably because it was a perfect night for running a 'coon. After he ate his supper, he strolled down to the bluff at the waterfall where so many times they had had a good race. He lay down to rest before going back up the hill to his house. As he rested, he thought about the pack. It had changed over the years. Old Drum had died, Blue was caught in an undertow on a flooded creek and drowned, and some of the others had left for other reasons. Belle had been his favorite of them all. She was a beautiful, sleek black and tan, and had visited him often after he had been adopted.

Suddenly he heard dogs running. When he heard Belle's bark he knew that it was his old pack. He knew that he would never fail to recognize her high-pitched lyrical bark. They were coming up the hollow straight to him. He stood and listened, continually sniffing the air for the familiar scent. As he listened to the progress of the race, he suddenly remembered another race in the same place. That time they were sure the 'coon was going to the big black gum den tree near the waterfall, and in their haste to head him off, he slipped by them and veered off to the right to another den, and the whole pack, including Red, overran the trail. By the time they had gone back and corrected their mistake, the 'coon was safely in his den. "This one will do the same thing," he thought as he ran down the hill. He hadn't gone far when he smelled the hot scent of the 'coon going just where Red thought he would. He started barking and following the trail, and the pack fell in behind him.

Just as he started up the last hill to the den tree, he felt a sudden, sharp pain in his chest. He fell and the pack ran past him—all but Belle, who was at the back of the pack, slowed now by aging muscles. Sensing that something was very wrong, she stopped and lay down beside him, licking his face, as his life ebbed away, and the rest of the pack raced away, trying to catch the 'coon.

All I could see was dead—gray and dead.

Frozen earth, leaden sky, trees stripped bare,

Boards on the old house long dead, now gray and decaying

Foundation stones standing like old grave markers.

## February

Desolation penetrated as deep as the cold wind,
  and deeper still.

Then as though it was only for me, to lift my sagging spirit,

There came the lilting, happy call of a red bird,

To remind me that springtime and resurrection are coming.

This is a photo of me and a buddy I sent home while in the service.
My words on the back are "we're not really that downhearted"

I was home on leave from the Air Force and wanted to hunt some. Dad and "N" Tollett had planned the hunt for me and told me to be ready about noon on Monday. Something came up and Dad couldn't go, so "N" picked me up, cautioning me to bring plenty of shells. I took a 16-gauge double barrel and plenty of shells, not thinking about extra clothes, because it was pretty warm. **Fall, 1956** We drove for quite a while, then stopped and hunted. "N" had a tree dog, and we killed three or four squirrels in the late afternoon. Instead of turning back towards Nashville, we went even farther away to a place they called "White Cliffs," to Bob Coleman's cabin. I had told Dena that it would probably be late when I got back, but I was surprised that we were going to eat supper at the cabin. After a supper of fried squirrel, gravy and biscuits, "N" got ready for bed, so I did too. Sometime in the night, it began to rain and was raining the next morning when we woke up. We lay in bed and talked a while, then "N" asked if I wanted to hunt in the rain — which I did. After breakfast, we started out.

The dog treed one in the first quarter of a mile, and I killed it. Then, within ten minutes, we had another. For the next two hours, that's the way it was. The squirrels were feeding on the ground everywhere we went. One time, the dog treed one in a tree-top that was laying on the ground. The squirrel wasn't ten feet from the ground when I killed it. One time, we had three running around in two trees, my shells were wet, the gun wouldn't eject the empty shells and "N" killed them all. I hadn't noticed, but for two hours, we had been going away from the cabin. When the squirrels quit moving, we were about three or four miles away. They quit moving when a really cold Northwest wind began blowing. By the time we got turned back and got the dog turned around, the wind was almost at gale force — and cold. I was carrying the 16 squirrels and didn't have a dry stitch on me. "N" had torn the game pocket of his old coat, couldn't carry any game and he was just as wet as I was. By the time we got back to the cabin, my hands were so numb I couldn't open the door with just one of them.

We finally got in, the dog went under the house to find him a bed in the leaves and we started taking off our wet clothes. I don't think that I have ever been so cold. "N" told me to put on a pot of coffee while he built a fire in the stove.

When the fire started, he dug around in an old quilt box and found us each a pair of one-piece long-johns and a pair of heavy, wool socks. We hung our wet clothes behind the stove, dried off as best we could with an old blanket, put on our underwear and socks, brought the coffee pot and put it on top of the stove and sat and drank the whole pot without getting up.

I have never before or since felt a fire that felt as good or tasted coffee that tasted like that did. Now, 50 years later, I can hear the cold wind howling, the fire popping, see the sides of the stove as it turned red from the heat and taste the coffee with canned milk in it. What a wonderful end to a perfect hunt!

A place where we made many a pot of coffee with Dad
and with Bob as well

Mother and Dad, always on a limited budget, could get us kids so excited about a simple cookout on some creek bank that the memories still linger almost 70 years later. The only expense to them was the gasoline it took to get there and back. The food we ate was exactly what we would have eaten at home, but it sure didn't taste the same. The event was so much fun and so exciting, that we remember it today. When Bobby

# Memories of Cooking Outdoors

would come home, he always wanted to have a cookout like we used to. Mother and Dad spent an entire day building a proper furnace on the old farm just for Bobby's cookout. We used this furnace a couple of times after Mom and Dad left us and we treasure those times.

All my memories I have of those earlier cookouts included fried potatoes, and fried cornbread patties. I can also remember salt meat, and onions, and peas and beans. If it was in the summer there would also be sliced tomatoes and green onions from the garden. I guess that we sometimes had fried fish that we had caught, something that we always planned on, but I don't remember it happening, though I'm sure it did.

I remember one time at Damascus when I was eight years old, that we kids, Marketa, Loweta, John, Bob, and I had a cookout down at the spring where grandfather's sorghum mill was. I wouldn't have remembered this campout if Marketa hadn't turned the cornbread too quick and scrambled it.

One time at Morrilton on Christmas day, Dad, John, Bob, and I went hunting on Point Remove creek. Mother fixed us a pot of coffee for Dad, and a pot of chocolate for us three boys. We built a fire and John heated up our drinks. I don't remember anything else about the hunt.

Grandfather Ward went with us one time to Cedar Creek in Perry County. He had a large blue speckled coffee pot which he filled about three-fourths full of water, put it on the fire and got it boiling, added the coffee to it and set it off the fire. In a little while he added a cup of cold water to settle the grounds, then let us drink some with Pet Milk in it. I have liked coffee since that time.

One time during deer season Dad found a hole of water where Cedar

Creek had changed its course and the next summer he took us there to fish. What I remember most about this trip was that Mom didn't want to quit fishing to cook lunch. The fish were biting whatever we threw at them and Mom was having the time of her life. We had a late lunch that day.

The past two years, John, Bill and I have gone to the woods on or near Dad's birthday, built a little furnace and made coffee. It is a special time for us as we remember Dad, and Bob, and Mother, and Butch, and Marketa and Suzy and a hundred other little cookouts that have meant so much to us.

Amazingly, Mom is not wearing her apron this time while trying her luck

**E**lmer was in a panic. His girlfriend Sally had placed herself in terrible danger. She was on the Joe Ward place, and though he called and called for her to stop, she went on. He had been nervous for a couple of weeks as the mating season approached. He had caught her two or three times cutting her eyes around at Fred, a beautiful eight pointer, and even at Josh, who was a big deer, but his antlers were all crooked (some said that it was caused by in-breeding).

Although there were many other females in the woods, everyone knew that Sally was his girlfriend reserved for him and no one else. They had pledged their love for each other, and he had vowed to protect her. But now she had entered the forbidden land, and he knew that the season was open for the deer hunters.

He had tried to get her to stop and chat as they strolled along through the Suzy Sanctuary, but she wasn't interested. He kept talking and walking along with her, until suddenly he was aware that they were walking directly into the forbidden land. The more he begged her to stop, the more she hopped gaily along, making a game of the whole thing. One time she turned around and said, "I think I'll go eat some corn from the Joe Ward feeder." He said, "You know that is forbidden except in the middle of the night," but still she continued on the forbidden land. Elmer would have simply turned around and deserted Sally, but he could not. She was his girl, one he had promised to protect. And what if Fred was over there in the Jenifer Preserve just waiting for Sally? He had told Fred in no uncertain terms that he would defend Sally even against him. Elmer only had six points on his antlers, but he was a perfect specimen, and even Fred knew that Elmer would be a formidable opponent. "Please, Sally, stop and come back here with me," Elmer called and called, but she seemed more determined than ever to defy him.

Finally, knowing that he had to follow, he tucked his tail down so he would be harder to see, then began slipping through the woods. Careful to make no noise, staying in the thickets as much as he could, heart pounding, nerves tingling, staying as low as he could, almost crawling, he passed the halfway point. He could now see the rock wall at the edge of the Jenifer Preserve. Only a few minutes more, and he told himself not to hurry. Then it happened. WHAM! He lunged into a headlong run, dodging the big trees, running over the little ones, desperate now to reach the rock wall. Then again, WHAM! Expecting to fall at any moment, with a tremendous surge of energy he reached the wall and leaped over it. SAFE AT LAST. He stopped, breathing hard, looking back, then another WHAM!

Now, he laughed at himself as he strolled along after Sally, for those were not gunshots, they were the big white oak acorns falling on the tin roof of the Joe Ward cabin.

T he leaf on the sweet gum tree was shaken awake by the sudden, sharp chill of the mid-September night. There had been other cool nights, but this was different. Wide awake now and with nothing to do but think, the words came back to him again, "You will mature into a full- grown, five-pointed, dark green leaf, live through the summer, and, when fall comes, you will die, fall off the tree

# The Leaf

and become fertilizer for the things that will grow next spring." These words had come from the mother tree back in the spring, but life was so good and full then that he had promptly put the words in the back of his mind. He had heard them again when he was a young adult as another leaf on his twig had lost his brightness, gradually turned yellow, then brown, and then one morning was gone, taken by the wind in the night. The mother tree had repeated the story again about dying and death and fertilizer, but with the weight of the dead leaf gone from his twig, he was lifted higher into a new group of playmates and life was better than ever. This was certainly no time to spend thinking about such sad things.

But now he had time. As he thought about the words, bitterness welled up in him. If there is a Supreme Being in charge of the whole universe, as he had always been told, why can't He run things better than this? And why was I born, if just to die? And if there is a God who could create me, why can't He just let me go on living? These bitter thoughts persisted during the days that followed, and he became irritable with the other leaves, the tree, the birds, and the universe itself.

With the arrival of Indian summer and its warm sunshine, he could almost forget the words again. But there was too much change around him. The black gum tree across the yard had turned a glowing red during the last few days, and the days were definitely shorter and the nights longer. The sun that had blistered him back in the summer now seemed to take forever to warm him in the mornings. The spots on his surface that had appeared a few weeks ago seemed to grow larger as he looked at them.

During the long sleepless nights, he reflected on the life behind him. He hadn't been the largest leaf on the tree, nor the topmost one, but he had been the largest on his twig, and what he lacked in size and position, he had made up for by being more aggressive than the others. He had produced his share of oxygen for the air-breathing creatures, though they hadn't seemed to notice. He had always provided all the shade he could for the grass and pets and the little girl. The little girl...that was a pleasant thought. She had come often to sit under him and read or play with her toys, and though the sun was blistering hot on him, he had stretched himself as flat as he could to shade her. And what was that she read over and over to memorize: "To everything there is a season and a time to every purpose under Heaven. A time to be born and a time to die; a time to laugh and a time to cry..." That said everything, didn't it? And everything would include a leaf, wouldn't it? Suddenly excited, he thought of the implications of this new revelation. If there is a plan so complex that it includes one leaf among countless millions of leaves, then it really must be some plan. It must have been conceived by the Supreme Being. "When I become food for the mother tree, I may become a part of her, since she grows a little each year. If I do that I will still be alive—just in another form."

As the day dawned after a night of these new thoughts, he looked around him. How differently things looked from a peaceful perspective. The colors around him were so beautiful he could hardly comprehend them. His own tree was such a bright yellow that it almost seemed to have a light inside it. He looked at the ground to see where he might fall. He'd not like to become fertilizer for that honeysuckle on the fence.

He spent the last of September and the first part of October watching the continual changes around him. He and his neighbors talked of the times past...the storm when they were young and how they had to cling for their lives to their twig, the hot dry times and then the refreshing rains. They also wondered aloud to each other about what the new buds would look like next spring.

Then one morning, as the dew lay heavy on him, a breeze came up, lifted him off the twig and sailed him gently over beside the honeysuckle. He wasn't aware, but his happiness would have been complete if he had known, that the little girl had seen his flight and had run and picked him up. She admired him a moment then laid him gently beside the mother tree.

H ere in the Fall of 2008 we are making our plans for next year when the doomsayers insist that we will be in a deep depression. By getting ready now, if it happens or doesn't happen we will be ready.

The garden is coming along nicely and will be ready to plant potatoes on Washington's birthday, or possibly the next day since his birthday falls on Sunday.

# Preparations for the Next Great Depression

This will be one of our major crops and we will plant plenty of them. We will grabble new potatoes for a while, then dig the rest. We will put the large ones on leaves under a tree, sprinkle some lime over them, then clean and can all the little ones to eat in the winter.

Much of this work will be done by family members who will arrive on their last tank of gas and will be responsible for four hours of "bread work" each day.

Our dairy operation will be at John's place, since he has plenty of pasture as well as a barn in which to do the milking. Be sure to bring any old bicycle you have to make travel faster between here and John's.

Someone will surely remember how to churn butter, and take care of that for all of us. We will build a chicken yard below the garden and hope that some of the hens will be inclined to "set" and raise some baby chicks. The cow will have had a new calf, and when it is big enough we will butcher it for those who can't live without an occasional burger.

The obvious place for our pork operation is at the pond in Cabin Village, however we are meeting some objections from Bill. We will try diplomacy to resolve this conflict.

John thinks that we will still have electricity and water, but if not then we will make some yokes that you can put on your shoulders and carry two buckets of water from the spring at the same time. Should some member of the group object to their assigned tasks, there is always the cleaning of the outhouses they can be assigned to.

At some point we will build a root cellar. This will be dug into a hillside, then poles laid across the top and dirt piled over it. Here we will store potatoes, carrots, turnips, sweet potatoes, squash, and if we do not have electricity we can keep our milk and butter there. When we kill hogs (if our pork plans don't fall through) we will render the lard since we won't have Crisco or oil to cook with and must use lard. Then next spring any lard left over can be used along with lye made from ashes to make soap.

The root cellar can also be used for a storm cellar, but if we don't have electricity we won't have television, so we won't know a storm is coming until it is here. We will have to learn to watch the skies and predict the weather.

Those who are accustomed to bathing more than once a week may have some difficulty. You will carry your water from the spring, heat it on the fireplace and pour it into a tub, all of which may get a little old. However the lye soap does such a thorough job, that once a week may be enough. Some of you may remember the song, "Grandma's Lye Soap:"

Do you remember grandma's lye soap,      Now little Herman and Brother Thurman
Good for everything in the home,      Had an aversion to washing their ears,
The dirty pans, the dirty dishes,      Grandma washed them with her lye soap,
It's for your hands and for your face.      And they haven't heard a word in years.


Of course her soap may have been a little strong on the lye.

We will probably not have fuel to operate our garden equipment, so the plowing will have to be human power. Perhaps some of the younger ones like Barry, Tony, Tim, Brian and Joey can pull the plow while some of us older ones can guide it, although Joey may be assigned to harvesting fresh meat most of the time.

All of these plans are of course subject to change, depending upon circumstances. Our lives will change, but it can be wonderful, if we have our attitude right. Think about the fun things, like showing your blisters and calluses, and telling how you milked a cow or fed the hogs, and how much free time you've saved up.

What a wonderful time we'll have.

**N**ovember, 1993—The stump of the oak tree on the corner of the lot is still there. It looks bad. Someone should have cut it down before now, but I'm glad they haven't. If they were interested in maintaining the look of the yard, they would have taken it down.

That tree was one of the clearest memories of Laurel. That was

# Laurel, Mississippi

where we played a lot in the summer. That was also the place where Bobby had an experience with a very irate lady whose car he ran into with a bicycle. I guess John told him everything he needed to know about riding a bicycle except how to stop one.

Bobby was probably six or seven years old. John got him started on his first ride by pushing him. Then when the crash occurred, John and I hid in the bushes in front of the porch while the lady talked to Bobby. As I remember, she was very angry, and he probably said, "Yes, Ma'am" several times.

It was on that porch, which was wider then than it is now, that I had my only birthday party. I was probably five. I remember kids coming. One girl, who was probably older than I, handed Mother my gift instead of giving it to me. She told Mother that I was jumping around like a puppy dog trying to get it.

Mother used to tell the story that on the morning of that birthday, I stood up in the bed and told her that my pants were too short since I had grown so much in the night. I don't remember that though.

I do remember her giving each of us a Carter's Little Liver Pill every night. None of us has had liver problems and that may be the reason. I remember being sent to sleep with Marketa the night Bill was born and the disappointment when he wasn't a girl. I think that it was better that he was a boy though. Some of the churches we sing in would probably not approve of a woman director.

The salesman who sold Mother the cookware with the little jiggling vent on the lids displayed it all on the floor just inside the living room door. Maybe the kitchen was messed up.

The railroad tracks are gone now but the right of way is there. The brick street is still there. That was the way the man would come in his wagon singing,

"Yes sir, no sir, don't mean maybe, we got watermelons for the baby. It's the watermelon man from the sandy land." I don't recall us ever buying from him, but he must have come by pretty often for me to remember him.

It seems like there were some people living kind of behind us named "Slaughter" where Mother sent me to borrow some vanilla flavoring. It smelled so wonderful that I tasted it on the way back. I remember how disappointed I was. I haven't tried it again.

The pasture we kept the cow in was a lot smaller that I remember. We had a half-barrel where water dripped from a hose all the time for her watering place. Near the back door were the giant elephant ears. The garage or storage building is gone. That was where John and Bob became interested in aerodynamics. They made a parachute from a tow sack and had me test it for them by jumping off the roof. I remember the bloody nose I got and the spanking they got.

The house is underpinned now, but it wasn't then. I shot John in the leg by shooting under the house and the BB stuck in his leg. I got in big trouble for that. I remember someone coming in the night and telling Dad that there was someone lying on the railroad tracks. Dad called the police who came and got him. He was drunk, and it was really exciting for us. Marketa, Loweta and John remember tramps walking down the tracks and coming to the house asking for a meal, and Mother feeding them on the back steps.

We left Laurel when I was six years old. A lot of things have changed, but the stump of the old oak tree is still there.

**H**arold Morse was working for me, I don't remember the year, and we got a contract for a larger house and needed some more help. Harold said that he knew a crew we could get, and he got them to come over. Jesse and Frank Blair and Silas Parks came and I hired them. We built that house and perhaps another, and when the others left I asked Si to stay on, and he did for a total **Silas Parks** of about 14 years. I have so many memories of that 14 years that I can't possibly write them all down, but I'll record some of them.

I learned early on that whatever we had to do, he could do it. And it never seemed to bother him if we were pouring concrete in the hot summer or putting the trim inside a house. It was all the same to him. In that 14-year period that he worked with me he was late for work three times. That would have been a fantastic record for someone living a block away from work, but he lived at Pleasant Valley, west of Bigelow. On two of those occasions there was a wreck on the river bridge that delayed him, and the other time he had to take someone to the hospital. Of course I knew in January every year that he would be gone the week that deer season opened.

Of all the men I've known, I have for the most part classified them as simply big men or small men. I have known rich, powerful men that were in my mind very small men. I have known men with several college degrees who held high positions who were very small men. And then I have known Si. He was small in stature, had no formal education, couldn't read a newspaper, but he had that rare quality that we call character, which made him one of my big men. One job that we did several years ago involved Si and the director of the Honors College at the University of Central Arkansas. The director of the college was also a big man and held a number of degrees, but he couldn't do what Si could do and Si couldn't do what he did. They worked together, the scholar and the carpenter, planning, discussing, laying out the remodeling of the building, each respectful of the other, and both happy with the result.

One time he turned in his time card at the end of the week and we found an error on it, where he had charged time to one job and it should have been another. We corrected it with no problem, but the following Monday he came to work earlier than normal, and told me that the reason he had made the mistake on his card was that he couldn't read. He said that he had brought my tools in because he was certain that I would let him go. I told him that it made no difference to me whether he could read or not, but that I was glad he had told me.

One Friday afternoon I went by his job and after we talked a while, I started to leave and told him that I would see him Monday. He said "we'll see you in a little while." This didn't sound right, so I said again that I would see him Monday, and again he said "we'll see you in a little while." I asked what he meant by a little while, and he said "Well, you didn't pay me this week, so I'm going to get the wife and kids and we're coming to your house." That was when I remembered that I had his paycheck in my pocket.

One time on a Friday afternoon we were working on some cabinets and he said, "Well, I guess you're going to Old House tonight." I said that instead of going to Old House that I was going to Little Rock to a poetry conference and quote some of my poetry to a bunch of people. He then asked me to quote him one of those poems. The poem I quoted was about a page long and I quoted the whole thing, a poem about a time I had been blind for a little while. He was putting varnish on the cabinets and he stopped with the brush up and listened, the varnish running down on his hand. When I finished, he started talking about the poem and in the next few minutes he had quoted back almost word for word at least half the poem.

One time he was painting something that I had built, and he said, "Well, if they ever outlaw caulking and putty, you're out of business."

One time we were replacing the floor joists that termites had eaten in a home in Conway, working our way across the living room when the owner came. He asked Si what he thought, and Si said, "We 'bout decided that they are eating ahead of us, we gonna cut a hole on the far side and see if we can head 'em."

He went home early a few times. If I didn't leave him enough to do to keep him all day, he would leave and not charge his time the rest of the day. Or if the weather was cold enough to freeze and it started raining or snowing he would leave immediately so he could be sure he would be able to get across the bridge. One time we were working on a job and it was cold and cloudy and someone built a fire in the fireplace of the house we were working on. He was outside and saw the ashes falling and started gathering up his tools ready to leave until someone told him that it wasn't snow.

His life revolved around his home and family, and was anchored by his wife Lillian. He would often say when we would be talking about our wives, "I sure got me a good woman."

"Don't ever get shooked about nuthin'" was one of his expressions that has served me well throughout the years since I first heard him say it.

The world didn't consider Silas Parks important. There were no big articles in the papers about his death. There were no dignitaries at his funeral, so to the world he wasn't important. But to his family and friends, the people who crowded the cemetery, he was important. He was important to every life his life touched. I will never forget him and the impact he had on my life. My life was made better because Si was a part of it.

The late artist George Fisher drew the little church for a fund-raising brochure

Here's the completed church which attracted quite a number
of worshippers when Dad was still preaching

A Christmas party at the church brought in every kid in the community

I was impressed with him the first time I saw him. Tall, angular, long arms and huge hands. I have large hands, but when we shook hands mine was swallowed up in his. I met him at church and then he called me to do some work on his home. He was always smiling it seemed, lots of teeth showing. Friendly, outgoing and outspoken. You always knew what he thought. We developed a friendship over the next few years, a relationship based on common values.

# Joe Dildy

Joe was born and raised in Nashville, Arkansas, and he and his brother were recruited along with Bear Bryant from Fordyce to play football for Alabama. They won the national championship in the Rose Bowl in 1935, a year after I was born. It was probably at Alabama that he developed his attitude toward winning. This attitude was dominant in his whole personality. One time I saw him coming into Nabholz Supply and told Danny Biddle at the sales desk to ask him if he agreed that it isn't whether you win or lose, but how you played the game. I got behind some shelves where he couldn't see me, and we listened to a 10-minute dissertation on winning. One thing he said was that anytime a game ended in a tie, that both teams had lost, no matter how well they played. He simply had no use for second best.

He didn't like "platoon" football or special teams. He didn't think it was real football. When he played, they played both ways, offense and defense. He played center, and with that build, those long arms and big hands, he was a formidable opponent. He maintained a close relationship with Bear Bryant, and made a number of trips to homecoming games, where he was sometimes honored at halftime. Whenever Alabama lost a game and I would give my condolences he would always say, "We'll be all right if we can beat Auburn." When he and Mary Ellen would travel to Alabama, they would pass the Arkansas State Prison, and he would always tell Mary Ellen, "There are four thousand innocent people out there, just ask them."

Arthritis took a toll on him in his last few years, and he fought it with the same intensity he had when he played football. War with an opponent, no holds barred. He called me to put a post in his carport near a step so he could hold on to it as he stepped up or down. I painted it for him, but it wasn't long before he had rubbed all the paint off and smoothed it down. His hand would almost wrap around a four by four post.

One time he hired us to tear down an old storage building and build a new one. He had an old Chevrolet pickup and insisted on hauling away the trash. We would start to help him load his truck, and he would tell us to build the new one, that he would handle the trash. By this time he was depending heavily on a walking cane, and he would drag a piece of lumber to the truck and somehow load it. One time he was dragging a piece of plywood with roofing on it and he fell with the plywood on top of him. We ran over to pick him up, and he said "Just roll me over and I can get up by myself." We did and he did, then pulled the trash to the truck, loaded it and took it to the dump.

His love and devotion to his wife Mary Ellen took center stage anytime I talked with him more than a few minutes. There was an almost child-like wonder in his eyes and his voice that someone as wonderful as she could have loved someone like him. Having known her for several years now, I think I understand what he meant.

My life has been made better because Joe and Mary Ellen have been a part of it.

T he man was born poor, and though he worked hard and was not a spendthrift, he remained poor. He lived on a rocky little hill farm, raised what he could and worked at a sawmill to feed his growing family. Then he lost his job. His boss told him that his work had been good, but the country was in a depression and there was no one to buy the lumber they produced, so the mill was closing. He walked all over the county looking for work, but everywhere he went he was told the same thing. "No work anywhere."

# The Man and the Mule

Although he was poor, he was also proud. He resolved that he would not let his family go hungry. He raised a big garden that year with a hoe and a shovel, breaking up the whole garden with a shovel, laying off the rows with a hoe. It took two weeks of back breaking labor to do this, because he had no mule to pull the plow. The last mule he had owned had stepped in a hole, broken a leg and had to be destroyed. His family did not go hungry that year, but it was a close thing. He had to have a mule. But a good mule would cost a hundred dollars and he didn't have even one dollar, and he didn't have a job.

Finally, one of his more prosperous neighbors offered to pay him thirty dollars to clear ten acres of land for him. It wasn't nearly enough money for the work, but he took the offer because there was nothing else. For four months he worked every day, cutting, burning, and clearing the land. When he was finished the neighbor paid him.

He took his money to the mule barn, though he knew that it wasn't nearly enough. He looked at the fat, sleek mules, but the cheapest one was ninety dollars. He turned to walk away, and the owner called him back and asked how much money he had. The man told him and the owner said that he had one old skinny mule in the back barn that he would sell for thirty dollars. The mule was so poor you could count his ribs, but he bought the mule, because that was all the money he had and he had to have a mule.

On the way home he decided that whoever had the mule before had starved him and that was why he was so poor. He decided that he would feed the mule all he would eat and he would get fat. When he arrived at home, his children quickly and properly named the mule, Ol' Skinny.

He began plowing the land, working 'Ol Skinny hard, because the ground was hard, and feeding him all he would eat every day. But Ol' Skinny stayed poor.

As the years went by, the times stayed hard, the rocky land stayed hard and the man too became hard, working his life away on the old land trying to feed his family. Through all those years the boy had never heard his daddy laugh, nor seen him cry, even at his own mother's funeral. He continued to work Ol' Skinny hard, but never abused him. He fed him all he would eat, but Ol' Skinny looked worse every year, and at the end of the seventh year, he died. With the help of a neighbor they dragged the carcass to the back of the pasture where the scavengers picked the bones clean.

In the winter of the year he died, the depression ended when the country became involved in a war. The man got his job back and could finally provide for his family.

The following summer on a Sunday afternoon the man and his son walked to the back of the pasture, and seeing the bones of Ol' Skinny they walked over to look at them. The man picked up the jaw bones and looked closely at them. He discovered that the two back teeth in the upper jaw had grown much too long, and had grown down behind the lower teeth and pressed against the jaw bone so hard that they had finally ground out holes all the way through. So that was why he stayed so skinny. He couldn't chew his food. In fact it would have been painful to even try. So he only ate enough to stay alive. The man cradled the bones in his hands and told the boy that he could have cut those teeth off, or pulled them out, if he had only known.

Then the hard old man knelt down on the hard old ground, and cried and begged forgiveness from a bony old mule who couldn't hear him, and it was the only time the boy ever saw his daddy cry.

**M**y lease was rapidly running out on the Old House farm where we were living, so I had to find a place to go. Up the road about a mile I located a farm with a two-bedroom house on it, with 157 acres of land. It also had two wells, a barn, one spring, two apple trees, a grapevine, a pecan tree, and other assets too numerous to mention. Being a bit short of money by this time, I bought it from the owner for $3000, paid

# The Happy Carefree Life of a Farmer

$500 down and agreed to pay the same amount per year until it was paid off. It was now late fall and we felt it desirable to have running water in the house. Actually, my wife said "Get it or live the happy, carefree life by yourself."

I spent the rest of the money I had making down payments on things like a bath set, water pump, butane tank, water heater, sink and septic tank. I installed everything as well as anyone I thought, until cold weather came and all my water pipes froze and burst. I replaced them off and on through the winter, but this didn't worry me too much, since I reasoned that the broken pipes would be ideal for irrigation next year, since I was going to be a modern farmer. Somewhere along the line I bought a tractor and various pieces of equipment. About the only thing I did with it was to plow up a small spot of land and plant turnips. I had read that during the depression people lived for months on nothing but turnips, and I wanted to be prepared for emergencies. The first time I went to harvest a mess, I saw cow tracks all over the field and found that my cows had harvested them for me. I know people had cows during the depression, but I guess they had better fences.

The pickup truck that had been so faithful during all the other problems now began to give out. It started with a transmission and ended with a motor and took some $300 out of our dwindling account. My brother Bill was now living with us and going to college in Conway, so we used his car whenever we wanted to go anywhere.

Living the happy, carefree life did not include starving. Dena and I each got a job in Conway. She went to work for an insurance company (this is significant) and with my training as a nuclear weapons mechanic, I got a job as a construction laborer. We all three came down each day in Bill's car until one day an oil line came off and we burnt up the motor. While the motor was being put in, I assessed our financial situation and found that our total assets were tied up in the cows. I sold them for a little less than I had paid for them (cattle had gone down) and paid for the motor.

I was now operating the farm on what was left over from the various payments and incidental expenses like groceries and gasoline. On a laborer's salary of $1.05 per hour this didn't leave a great deal, but I decided that I could sow about 40 acres of soil building grass on some land I wanted to use for pasture in the future. Since I now had no cows, all pasture plans were for the future. A lot of the farmers in the area made it a practice to just sow the seed on top of the ground and let it go at that, but I decided that since I had a tractor, I would do it right. I would break and disc the land to prepare a proper seed bed, which I proceeded to do. A lot of people have problems with the power lift on their tractors, but their problems are that it won't lift the implement. My problem was that it wouldn't let it down. The local shade tree mechanics couldn't handle this kind of problem, and though I tried, I couldn't figure it out either. I solved the problem by leaving the lift down and turning in large circles. In the end, I decided to just throw the seed on top of the ground and let it go at that.

Somewhere along the line, Bill's car had been sold to pay for something like registration or something, and since we had to have dependable transportation, I traded the truck in on a newer model. It was a 1957 Ford with a custom cab and after riding in the old truck it felt like a Cadillac. I bought new rear tires for it with mud and snow tread on them and about the time I got them put on it started to snow. I put a few sticks of wood in the back for added traction and went to work and back just fine, but when we got home, one of them was flat. I put the spare on which was naturally slick and that night Bill had to go back to school for something. He had Dad's car up there and since the tire on the truck was slick, we decided that he should take Dad's car. He got about a mile and turned it over into a deep ditch. The next day I got a man to pull it out for $25. This money came from the grocery fund, so we decided to kill one of the hogs. This we did without incident except for the fact that I didn't know exactly where a hog's brain was and shot it too low and we had to chase it down and shoot it again.

We made it through the winter, our first one on the farm, in pretty good shape except for the incidents mentioned and for the fact that we owed somewhere in the neighborhood of 2,500 dollars.

One bright spring morning in April, a Saturday, we got up early and planted the garden. We planted potatoes, onions, radishes, and lettuce. We went back to the house feeling that we finally had the world by the tail on a downhill pull and seated ourselves to a breakfast of ham, eggs, and hot biscuits. We should have had a premonition right then of things to come, for Dena didn't make biscuits very often. I had taken the trash out and set it on fire and came back to eat. The next time someone looked out, the field north of the house was on fire. I got the tractor and started plowing around it and Bill was fighting it with a wet sack. I was making some headway with the plowing when I looked back towards the house and saw that it was on fire. We got a few things out and the rest burned along with the rest of the house.

We had no insurance, which was embarrassing for Dena when the article came out in the paper, stating that we had no insurance and in the next sentence gave the name of the insurance company where she worked. We moved into an apartment in Conway and began paying off the things that we had made down payments on. I called the credit department of the company we had bought everything from, told the lady what had happened, and she said that if I would say that none of the things had been installed, she would write off the balance. I declined that lie, and over the next two years we paid it all off. We're all square now and steadily building up our courage and resources for another shot some day at the happy, carefree life of a farmer.

Dad lighting the lanterns at the brush arbor,
and posing at the tree stump pulpit

Getting ready for services in the brush arbor.
Amos Brown on the left, Aud Shofner with his
hand on his chin. Both are deceased

**S**mooth cloudy days when the wind is from the northwest and the daytime temperature stays in the fifties.

Sparkling clear mornings with frost that Dad would say looks like a young snow.

Mental images of Mom with her old red-checked coat with a rag of some kind tied over her ears going to the barn.

# Things I Like to Remember

The smell of gun oil and hunting clothes, and shotgun shells that said "Peters packs the power."

The smell of wet fallen leaves, and the smell of burning leaves.

The sound of old Queen barking, and Dad explaining that she was trailing or treed, and sometimes whether it was a gray or fox squirrel that she was after.

The sound of water hitting the ground when a squirrel jumps and hits a limb.

The feel in the air when the weather really cools off in the fall.

Driving home in the late afternoon when it has been raining and now the wind is blowing and it seems that all the leaves are falling at once.

Going squirrel hunting with Dad, and him getting on to me because I couldn't see the squirrel up in the big white oak, and him saying that it looked like a piece of red flannel up on that limb.

Gathering everything in the garden that is ripe and taking it in for Mom to can soup mixture. And the next winter her taking a half gallon jar of it, putting it in a big pot, then adding whatever else she thought it needed, cooking it all afternoon and serving it for supper with a pan of hot cornbread.

Fishing in the early fall at Scroggins Creek when lots of leaves had fallen on the water.

All of us going to Shaw bottom, Dad and the older boys hunting, Mom and all the little ones picking up hickory nuts.

Peanuts pulled and turned upside down to dry.

Picking cotton and finding a watermelon and eating it.

Going night hunting with Dad and "N" Tollett.

Booger, Bill, and me hunting at Mom and Dad's place before they moved up there.

Getting a fresh drink of water at the end of a long day of working in the fields with only lukewarm water to drink.

Hog killing.

The smell of dirt being turned by a plow in the spring.

The rustling sound of dry corn stalks being blown by the wind in the early winter.

Coming in the house from "doing up the work" in the winter—ears, hands and feet frozen, bringing a steaming bucket of milk and the eggs into a warm room filled with the smells and sounds of supper ready to go on the table.

Grandpa's sorghum mill at Damascus, and all the memories connected with it including hot biscuits, country butter and hot syrup.

Leftover food under the tablecloth on the kitchen table.

Daddy waking us up in the middle of the night at Morrilton to show us the eight inches of snow on the ground, and trying to get back to sleep.

Going hunting at Shaw bottom in the snow, tracking a 'possum into a hollow log and twisting it out.

Being at Old House alone and John or Bill coming in.

Going hunting and tracking with Dad in fresh snow.

Getting fish bait. Mom and Dad could get us so excited about going fishing that we would work for hours digging worms. Sometimes we would stop on the way and seine a water hole or a branch for crawfish and little perch.

Mom taking any of the grandkids that were there and going fishing down at the pond.

Coming in from quail hunting with dad and a coat full of birds, knowing how they would taste when mom got them fried and made biscuits and cream gravy.

Going swamp rabbit hunting on the Arkansas River with Dad, John, Bob, and Pem Shofner. Mom would take these big rabbits, cut them up, brown them in the pressure cooker, then add water, potatoes, onions and Worchestershire sauce and pressure cook them for a while and then serve them with hot biscuits. I can close my eyes and almost taste that food now.

Uncle Carl, John, Bob, and me going wood-cutting at Needs Creek, taking lunch to cook, all piled in the "Hoopie" we called it. Uncle Carl wasn't supposed to eat anything fried or any pickles. We fried potatoes, salt meat, cornbread, and had a jar of pickles. He ate more than any of us.

The last day of school in the Spring, and the feeling of complete freedom. Which would end the next day when I started working in the fields.

The last day of school before the Christmas holidays. Thoughts of hunting, the excitement of Christmas.

Heading out to the squirrel woods with Dad

**W**hat I would really like to do today is go back—to the farm, to Mother and Dad's house. In my mind, this is what I would do.

I would greet them as always, but this time I would tell them how much I loved them and what they meant to me. I would place my hands on each of their shoulders and look them straight in the eye so they could not fail to understand what I was saying. I would say "I love you, I appreciate you and the way you have raised me." I would tell them that they taught me right from wrong, what a family is supposed to be.

## If I Could Go Back

To Mom, I would say that "You gave me your eternal optimism, your love for the outdoors, the little flowers in the spring, the love of growing things, your outlook on life."

To Dad I would say that "You taught me the love of the outdoors, you taught me sportsmanship, the thrill of finding game, as well as the fun of simply being in the outdoors whether we killed any game or caught any fish, and you taught me to dream of things that I might someday do or be."

You both taught me the love of reading, the joy I could find in a good book. Mom, you taught me that there was something good in everyone, and not to criticize others, because there was some reason they acted like they did. I would tell Mom and Dad that the most important thing they taught me was that there was a God, that He loved me, and how to trust Him. They taught me what faith is and how important it is in my life.

I would take a couple of rose bushes for Mom and plant them for her, something in a color which would compliment her Mr. Lincoln. I would go with Dad down to the pea patch and we would pick a bushel of peas for shelling later on when it would be cooler and we could sit on the front porch. While Mom fixed dinner (at noon of course), I would go with Dad in Old Smoothmouth (the name Dad assigned to his ancient pickup truck) down in the woods and help him cut a load of firewood for winter. When we came back to the house I would take a few minutes to pet and scratch Old Queen and tell her what a wonderful dog she was, though she wouldn't understand. I would go with Mom to the orchard and we would gather some apples, take them to the house, peel and slice them and put them on the storm cellar roof to dry. By this time it would be cool enough on the porch to sit and shell the peas that Dad and I had picked. Late in the afternoon, Preacher Rabbit would come out from under the study and Dad would turn loose Roxey and Rosie (his Beagles) and let them chase Preacher Rabbit for a while until he went back under the study. Then I would insist that Mom sit down with her book while I cleaned up the kitchen.

I would tell them again that I loved them and then I would go home.

If I could go back

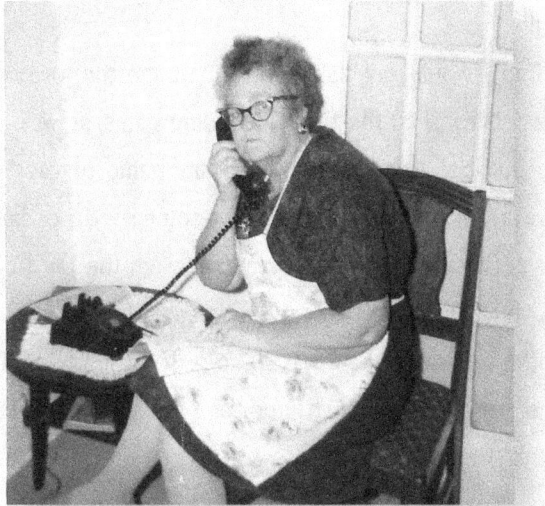

Mom in a listening mode on the phone

# My Brother Joe

**H**e defies description, more than any person I have known. Independent to a fault, yet strongly attached to his family and friends, anxious to share the beauties of nature to all who will listen, greatly excited when he finds a brace of really meaty ham hocks in the store, his mind moving toward a pot of beans or perhaps cornmeal dumplings.

A passion for cooking country food, and really good at it — vegetables from the garden, wonderful biscuits and/or cornbread, depending on what else he sets out, and the visible pleasure as we eat up everything with gusto.

Joe is the third of five brothers and the fifth of eight children born to Roy and Mamie Ward. He is a veteran, and a patriot, all the way through. It marks his conversation, his view of current events and his likes and dislikes, clearly stated and not afraid of hearing contrary opinions so he can further prove that he won't be changing his mind.

Joe is a dreamer, always has been, and writes about it in this book, some of those dreams crashing on the rocks of reality. One dream realized was to build a cabin near the old home place which he keeps ever present in his memory and brings into most conversations at one point or another. The cabin, when it was completed (and even before) became the focal point of his life, and he managed to crunch around his work schedule so he could be at the cabin from Thursday night through Saturday on just about every weekend.

He is devoted to his wife of 55 years, Dena, and their children Joey and Mica. And he welcomes the grandchildren and great-grandchildren to the cabin whenever they can come visit. Dena is there most weekends with him. She enjoys those times at the cabin, in part because Joe loves it so and also because she isn't that far from her own roots.

Entertaining is part of their programming and Joe will cook a late Saturday breakfast for 15 or 20 friends at the drop of a hat.

He enjoys telling them stories, sometimes reading what he has written and letting them see how immersed he is in the lives of those who have gone before. Joe has an enviable ability to recall details from his own past and from the lives of his parents and grandparents, and those events too find their way into his stories.

Joe argues that he is not a writer but the reader of these stories will undoubtedly beg to differ.

He has had some health setbacks, although he seems to be fine now; but he got more closely in touch with his own mortality from all that, and with the urging of his wife and his two brothers – John and Bill – who share Black Hill Road with him, he set about to get all his stories into print. He asked John and Bill to help him, since both came to the project with much experience and background. Bill had just published a beautiful book of his own about Conway and John is the author of two books about Winthrop Rockefeller plus assorted other published writings during and after his stint as managing editor of the daily newspaper in Conway. Joe's praise of their efforts on his behalf has been effusive, to say the least, and it is a fact that both brothers have given the project their full and enthusiastic attention and support to get it done.

The results of that are here for all to see.

—John L. Ward

www.ingramcontent.com/pod-product-compliance
Lightning Source LLC
LaVergne TN
LVHW021522080426
835509LV00018B/2604